Gold
EXPERIENCE

B1+

Pre-First for Schools

Vocabulary
and Grammar
Workbook

Sheila Dignen

Contents

01	Inside or outside?	4
	Revision Unit 1	8
02	Making it happen	10
	Revision Unit 2	14
03	True story?	16
	Revision Unit 3	20
04	Things they don't teach you	22
	Revision Unit 4	26
05	Green world	28
	Revision Unit 5	32
06	Before time	34
	Revision Unit 6	38
07	The feel-good factor	40
	Revision Unit 7	44
08	Magic numbers	46
	Revision Unit 8	50
09	All change	52
	Revision Unit 9	56
10	Inspiration	58
	Revision Unit 10	62
11	The art of make-believe	64
	Revision Unit 11	68
12	Find your voice	70
	Revision Unit 12	74

VOCABULARY

1 Unscramble and write the adjectives related to work and skills.

1   *part-time* (trap-mite)
2   _____ (erlaxngi)
3   _____ (lelw-daip)
4   _____ (eassnoal)
5   _____ (lulf-mite)
6   _____ (ewraridng)
7   _____ (isatsfygni)
8   _____ (sessrtluf)

2 Complete the sentences with adjectives related to work and skills.

1   Working in a busy restaurant can be very s*tressful* _____ sometimes.
2   My mum only works in the mornings, so she doesn't work f_____ .
3   A lot of work on farms is s_____ , because there isn't much to do in the winter.
4   My brother loves money, so he definitely wants a w_____ job in the future.
5   I enjoy tidying my room – it's very s_____ to see it looking nice.
6   He's looking for a p_____ job, just two or three days a week.
7   Babysitting is quite a r_____ job when the children are asleep!
8   I guess teaching is a r_____ job when you can see that the children are learning.

3 Choose the correct answers.

1   We're (making)/doing/getting plans for our summer holidays.
2   Our boss puts/keeps/has an eye on us all the time.
3   Sam couldn't be a builder. He hates getting/ making/having his hands dirty!
4   You need to wear warm clothes when you're working out/outdoor/outdoors.
5   I don't think I could cope for/with/to being the boss.
6   I'd like to make/prove/give to myself that I can do this job.

4 Complete the adjectives with the missing vowels.

1   f _a_ sh _i_ o n _a_ bl _e_
2   _____ n c r _____ d _____ bl _____
3   c _____ m f _____ rt _____ bl _____
4   t _____ r r _____ bl _____
5   s _____ n s _____ bl _____
6   _____ n d _____ r s t _____ n d _____ bl _____
7   r _____ l _____ bl _____

5 Complete the job advert with these words.

> flexible   organised   practical   punctual
> reliable   ~~responsible~~   suitable

Assistant Zoo Keeper

We are looking for a part-time helper at the zoo. You must have the following qualities:
You must be 1) *responsible* , and take your work seriously.
You must be 2) _____ and arrive on time for work.
You must be 3) _____ and able to keep your workplace tidy.
You must be a 4) _____ person, who's good at dealing with problems and deciding what is possible in different situations.
You must be 5) _____ , as the working hours change each week.
You must be a 6) _____ person, because we need someone that we can trust.
If you think you are 7) _____ for this job, please email us at the address above.

6 Look at the pictures and write the words.

1 _hoodie_
2
3
4
5
6
7
8

7 Find eight words for clothes and accessories. The words go across, down or diagonally. The first letter of each word is highlighted.

w	c	a	j	k	i	p	l	u	r	o
e	a	o	e	p	i	a	f	r	n	u
a	s	t	w	l	y	t	l	a	r	t
t	u	g	e	f	l	e	a	b	s	f
t	a	r	l	r	v	o	t	a	c	i
y	l	o	l	a	p	i	s	t	o	t
h	y	h	e	m	i	r	h	e	a	l
j	s	t	r	i	p	y	o	r	t	p
w	o	r	y	y	i	b	e	o	r	t
b	a	g	g	y	m	l	s	a	f	e

8 Match the adjectives for describing clothes (1–7) with the definitions (a–g).

1 stripy
2 baggy
3 tight
4 spotty
5 plain
6 casual
7 patterned

a with any kind of pattern
b fitting close to your body
c with no pattern
d with a pattern of lines
e not fitting close to your body
f with a pattern of small circles
g not formal

9 Unscramble and write the words for clothes and accessories.

1 She wears a lot of _jewellery_ (ejewrlley), like rings and necklaces.
2 Your new _____ (ahriystle) really suits you.
3 I think you worry about your _____ (migea) too much!
4 At school, we wear a jumper with the school _____ (gool) on it.
5 I sometimes wear a _____ (itwrsabdn) on my arm when I play tennis.
6 I like your new hat and _____ (csraf).
7 He often wears a hoodie and some _____ (rtacktuis tombots).
8 I never buy expensive _____ (neresdig bella) clothes.

10 Read the article and choose the correct answer, A, B, C or D.

The best job!

I think my job is the most 1) _____ job in the world! I'm a water-slide tester! Of course, this job isn't for everyone. It's 2) _____, so you can't work all-year round. And you have to cope 3) _____ getting wet all the time! But I think it's great. It's never 4) _____, because you feel as if you're on holiday all the time! And you don't have to worry about what to wear to work, because there's only one possible 5) _____ - your swimming costume! I must admit that it isn't a very 6) _____ job, but then money isn't everything. Although it's fun, you do have to be 7) _____ and concentrate on what you're doing. And you need to 8) _____ an eye on your speed, because it can be dangerous if you go too fast!

1 A satisfy B satisfying
  C satisfied D satisfies
2 A monthly B annual
  C seasonal D partial
3 A for B of
  C to D with
4 A stress B stressful
  C stressed D stressfully
5 A outfit B clothes
  C logo D suit
6 A generous B rich
  C well-paid D wealthy
7 A sensitive B right
  C carefully D sensible
8 A keep B have
  C get D put

GRAMMAR
Present tenses

1 Choose the correct answers.

1 My brother *always is/is always/is always being* late for school!

2 Jamie *doesn't wear/isn't wearing/isn't wear* a hoodie today.

3 The price of clothes *is getting/gets/are getting* higher and higher.

4 I *don't often see/don't see often/am not often seeing* my friends at the weekend.

5 I'm sorry, I *am not understand/don't understand/am not understanding* this.

6 My dad *tells always/always tells/is always telling* me I should study more. It's so annoying!

7 We can't play tennis, because it *rains/is rain/is raining* at the moment.

8 I *enjoy always/am always enjoying/always enjoy* music lessons at school.

2 Write sentences in the present simple or the present continuous.

1 Sam / play / tennis / at the moment
Sam is playing tennis at the moment.

2 my brother / always / borrow / my things

3 I / usually / do / my homework / after dinner

4 they / live / in London / ?

5 my friends / wait / for me / right now

6 where / you / go / ?

7 it / often / sunny / in July

8 the hero / jump / out of the aeroplane

3 Complete the sentences with the present simple or present continuous form of these verbs. Include the adverbs where they are given.

always / be   always / use   live   look after
make   ~~never / get up~~   not study   watch

1 I _____*never get up*_____ before nine o'clock on Saturday mornings.

2 I don't want to come out at the moment. I _____ a movie on TV.

3 Joe _____ happy when his team wins!

4 (you) _____ in New York?

5 My sister _____ my phone. It really annoys me!

6 We _____ German this year.

7 (you) _____ your baby sister today?

8 This week we _____ plans for our summer holidays.

4 Complete the email with one word in each space.

mailbox   Today | Mail | Calendar | Contacts

Reply | Reply All | Forward | Delete

To: **Jenna**   Subject: **I'm bored!**

Hi Jenna,
What 1) _____*are*_____ you doing? 2) _____ you want to come round to my house? I'm 3) _____ doing anything interesting 4) _____ the moment, and there isn't anything interesting on TV, 5) _____ usual! If you 6) _____ free now, maybe we can get together tomorrow or 7) _____ the weekend? I 8) _____ have any plans yet. My cousin is 9) _____ telling me I should go to the new cinema in town. Maybe we should do that.
See you soon,
Anja

Articles

5 Choose the correct answers.

1 My cousin lives in *USA/the USA*.
2 *Money/The money* isn't very important to me.
3 Did you watch that documentary on *the TV/TV*?
4 Do you want to go to *cinema/the cinema* today?
5 *Life/The life* can be difficult sometimes.
6 He wants to climb *Mount Everest/the Mount Everest*.
7 We swam in *Pacific Ocean/the Pacific Ocean*.
8 My brother doesn't have a job, so he's looking for *work/the work*.

6 Complete the conversations with *a*, *an* or *the*.

A Do you want to go to 1) *the* theatre tonight?
B Yes, and why don't we go to 2) _____ restaurant first, for 3) _____ meal?
A Good idea. We can go to 4) _____ Italian restaurant I went to last week. It's very nice.

A Can I borrow 5) _____ pen, please?
B Where's 6) _____ pen I lent you last week?

A Excuse me, is there 7) _____ bank near here?
B Yes. There's one next to 8) _____ police station.

A Have you got 9) _____ new phone?
B Yeah. It was 10) _____ birthday present.

7 Choose the correct answer, A, B or C.

1 There were more than _____ people at the concert.
  A thousand B thousands C a thousand
2 Trains are a very popular form of _____ .
  A transport B a transport C the transport
3 I usually see my friends three _____ week.
  A times B times a C times the
4 There's a really good shoe shop on _____ .
  A the North Street
  B a North Street
  C North Street
5 My brother's at _____ .
  A Bristol University
  B a Bristol University
  C the Bristol University
6 We waited for three and _____ hours!
  A half B a half C the half
7 My mum always reads _____ magazine.
  A *Vogue* B the *Vogue* C a *Vogue*
8 We visited _____ in London last week.
  A National Gallery
  B the National Gallery
  C a National Gallery

8 Underline the mistake in each sentence.

1 I'd love to visit the South America.
2 I love music, but I'm not very interested in the art.
3 I'm reading the very interesting book right now.
4 We go out for a meal once the week.
5 Paris is the capital city of a France.
6 The plane leaves from a Heathrow Airport.
7 They climbed the Mount Kilimanjaro with a guide last summer.
8 Do you prefer watching TV or going to theatre?

9 Complete the article with *a*, *an*, *the* or –.

No hoodies?

A lot of young people wear hoodies, but there's 1) *a* shopping centre in Kent, in 2) _____ UK, where hoodies aren't allowed. 3) _____ shopping centre decided to stop teenagers wearing hoodies from coming in because some older customers found them frightening. Jack, 4) _____ teenager from the town, is angry. 'It's not fair. I always met my friends here before,' he says. 'There's 5) _____ nice café where we met and we went to 6) _____ cinema here once or twice 7) _____ week. Now we can't do that.' Now Jack and his friends are taking 8) _____ advice from a lawyer and hope that they can make 9) _____ shopping centre think again!

Revision Unit 1

1 Complete the table with the correct form of the word given.

Verb	Noun	Adjective
relax	–	1) _relaxing_
suit	–	2)
satisfy	–	3)
–	sense	4)
–	stress	5)

2 Choose the correct answer, A, B or C.

1 Mark doesn't like _____ his hands dirty.
   A having   **(B)** getting   C making
2 I don't think Jo will _____ with this job.
   A cope   B enjoy   C achieve
3 I want to prove _____ myself that I can do it!
   A for   B with   C to
4 He asked me to keep _____ on the young animals.
   A eyes   B my eyes   C an eye
5 We're busy _____ plans for next year.
   A making   B doing   C getting
6 You're going to be in a movie? That's _____!
   A terrible   B incredible   C suitable
7 Mia isn't _____ enough to do that job.
   A comfortable   B suitable   C responsible
8 We had a great holiday but the weather was _____.
   A terrible   B flexible   C incredible

3 Complete the sentences with one word in each space.

1 You wear w_aterproo_f clothes to protect you from the rain.
2 You wear an a_____n to keep your clothes clean when you're cooking.
3 A h_____e is a top that has a part to cover your head.
4 Wearing g_____s keeps your hands warm.
5 You wear g_____s to protect your eyes when you are skiing or swimming.
6 Your h_____e is the way your hair is cut and shaped.
7 A s_____-s_____ shirt has sleeves that only cover the top part of your arms.
8 You wear a s_____f around your neck to keep you warm.

4 Complete the sentences with these words.

> baggy   designer label   flip-flops   ~~image~~
> kit   necklace   outfit   plain

1 I'm careful about choosing clothes because my _image_ is quite important to me.
2 I prefer _____ clothes. I hate clothes that are too tight!
3 I bought a smart new _____ for my job interview.
4 Do you like Manchester United's new _____?
5 Do you prefer _____ T-shirts or patterned ones?
6 Oh, what a lovely gold _____!
7 I've got a pair of _____ to wear at the beach.
8 I can't afford to buy _____ clothes!

5 Complete the sentences with the correct form of the words in capitals.

1 I wear _comfortable_ shoes when I'm working, because I'm on my feet a lot. **COMFORT**
2 I think that teaching is a very _____ job. **REWARD**
3 Rob was wearing a _____ shirt and a plain tie. **STRIPE**
4 I bought a _____ summer dress. **SPOT**
5 I think it's _____ that Paula was upset. **UNDERSTAND**
6 You have to be very _____ to do this job. **ORGANISE**
7 He wants to pass his exams so that he can get a well-_____ job when he leaves school. **PAY**
8 You must work _____ hours in this job. **FLEX**
9 You must prove to _____ that you can succeed with this project. **YOUR**
10 Sam is a very _____ worker. You can always depend on him. **RELY**

6 **Complete the sentences with the present simple or present continuous form of the verbs in brackets.**

1 I _____*usually get*_____ (usually / get) home from school at 4.30.

2 I _____ (not see / often) my cousins because they live in Canada.

3 My dad is very busy. He _____ (work) really hard at the moment.

4 In the film, Oliver _____ (go) to New York to find work.

5 I think it _____ (become) more and more difficult for young people to find work.

6 My sister _____ (always / wear) a uniform to work.

7 I _____ (try) to be more careful with my money at the moment.

8 My mum is really annoying. She _____ (always / tell) me I don't work hard enough!

9 I'm sorry, I _____ (not agree) with you.

10 This is a great party! I _____ (enjoy) it!

7 **Rewrite the sentences correctly.**

1 Jack always is late!
   Jack is always late!

2 We buy usually our lunch in the canteen.
   _____

3 What do you do at the moment?
   _____

4 I play tennis most weekend.
   _____

5 I'm watching TV at moment.
   _____

6 I often don't cycle to school.
   _____

7 My sister always is borrowing my things!
   _____

8 I'm sorry, I'm not understanding you.
   _____

8 **Complete the sentences with *a*, *an*, *the* or –.**

1 Would you like __*a*__ biscuit?

2 _____ work doesn't have to be boring – it can be fun!

3 I saw _____ really good film last night.

4 My uncle lives in _____ Australia.

5 Look, there's _____ boy I told you about.

6 We usually go on holiday once _____ year.

7 I'd love to go to _____ Bahamas!

8 They sailed down _____ Amazon in a small boat.

9 My brother wants to go to _____ Harvard University.

10 I bought this dress in _____ Harrods.

9 **Complete the email with one word in each space.**

| mailbox | | Today | Mail | Calendar | Contacts |

Reply | Reply All | Forward | Delete

To: **Sara**   Subject: **My new job!**

Hi Sara,
How are you? I started 1) __*a*__ part-time job last week. I'm working in 2) _____ café in York. I only work for about six and 3) _____ half hours a week, but it's good to have some money! 4) _____ you still looking for a job? I 5) _____ think they want any more waiters here 6) _____ the moment, but I can let you know if anyone leaves. 7) _____ café here is really nice. It 8) _____ serve main meals – just drinks and snacks. You could come in and see me at work. It's OK, you 9) _____ have to buy anything!
Hope to see you soon,
Georgia

02 Making it happen

VOCABULARY

1 Complete the crossword with technology words.

```
1                              2
H                              [ ]
A        3
         [ ]
4
C        [ ]
                    5
K                   [ ]
                    [ ]
                           6
                           [ ]
7
[ ]
```

Across

3 to move information from the internet onto a computer or smartphone

4 a set of instructions that tell a computer what to do

5 to add more information to something

6 a set of instructions that can damage a computer

7 a group of documents that you store together on a computer

Down

1 to secretly get information from someone's computer

2 an object that provides a supply of electricity for a device such as a smartphone

3 to remove something that is stored on a computer

2 Choose the correct answers.

1 Did you read Sara's *tweet*/*signal* about her party?

2 It's a very useful application and you can download the *connection*/*software* for free.

3 I've just got a new *touch screen*/*virtual* phone.

4 I couldn't call you earlier, because I couldn't get a *signal*/*connection* for my phone.

5 John plays lots of *online*/*click* computer games.

6 My sister spent £5 on food for the animals in her *program*/*virtual* zoo!

7 It takes ages to download things because the internet *website*/*connection* is so slow!

8 Allgames.com is a great *online*/*website* for games.

3 Complete the sentences with the correct form of these verbs.

> access   charge   click   ~~delete~~   download
> hack   scroll   update

1 I was so annoyed! I accidentally ___*deleted*___ my essay from my computer, so I had to write it again!

2 I forgot to _____ my phone last night, and now it's out of battery!

3 If you _____ down the page, you'll see more information at the bottom.

4 These files are protected, so you need a password to _____ them.

5 If you _____ on that icon, the program will open.

6 Listen to this song – I _____ it onto my phone yesterday. Do you like it?

7 The school website hasn't got any information about this term's events yet. They need to _____ it.

8 Someone _____ into the bank's computer last night and stole information about customers' accounts.

4 Match the sentence beginnings (1–6) with the endings (a–f).

1 I'm going to follow up ___*c*___

2 I'm still trying to work out _____

3 You need a password to log on _____

4 You have to key in _____

5 Can you zoom in _____

6 You'll save energy if you turn off _____

a to the website.

b your name and then press 'Enter'.

c your idea of trying to get a summer job.

d on that picture, so we can see it better?

e your computer at night.

f the answer to this maths problem.

5 Read the definitions and write the words.

1 a machine that prints documents _printer_
2 a device that transmits a signal ....
3 a machine that scans documents ....
4 someone who collects things ....
5 someone who competes ....
6 someone who invents things ....
7 someone who plays a game ....
8 someone who instructs people how to do something ....

6 Complete the table with the correct noun forms.

Verb	Noun
receive	1) _receiver_
amplify	2) ....
generate	3) ....
photocopy	4) ....
advise	5) ....
refrigerate	6) ....
program	7) ....
narrate	8) ....

7 Complete the sentences with nouns formed from these verbs.

> amplify calculate collect employ
> generate instruct invent photocopy
> play refrigerate

1 The meat is all stored in a _refrigerator_ to keep it cool and fresh.
2 Jo dreams of being a professional football .... one day.
3 The music isn't loud enough for this big hall. We need an .... to make it louder.
4 When you go for a job interview, you should try to impress your future ....
5 We had a really good ski .... who taught us a lot about skiing.
6 I can't do this maths in my head. Can I borrow your ....?
7 The school has its own .... to produce electricity if there's a power cut.
8 Who was the .... of the first computer?
9 My uncle's a .... of model aeroplanes. He's got over thirty!
10 Can I use your ....? I need to make a copy of my passport.

8 Complete the sentences with the correct form of the verbs in brackets. Use re- or dis-.

1 Jack was here a few minutes ago, but he's _disappeared_ (appear) now!
2 I spilled water on my homework, so I had to .... (do) it!
3 I'm sorry, but I .... (agree) with you. I think you're wrong!
4 Can you .... (play) that song? I love it.
5 I didn't understand the text about technology. I had to .... (read) it several times.
6 My grandad .... (approve) of new technology, and he refuses to go near a computer!
7 The band couldn't get the song right, so they decided to .... (record) it the next day.
8 I wouldn't dare to .... (obey) my parents! They would be furious!
9 Sara's really nice – I can't understand why you .... (like) her!

9 Complete the fact sheet with the correct form of the words in brackets.

Music, TV and Radio

Did you know...?

- The first electric 1) _amplifier_ (amplify) was invented in 1909 by Lee De Forest. Without him, there would be no rock concerts!
- The first portable music 2) .... (play) went on sale in the 1960s. It used small cassettes, with recorded music on.
- Alan Blumlein was the 3) .... (invent) of stereo sound, the system that directs different sounds through different speakers. He invented it in 1931.
- The first radio 4) .... (receive) was designed by Alexander Popov in 1896, but people didn't start having radios in their homes until the early 20th century.
- The first TV 5) .... (transmit) was developed by John Logie Baird in London in the 1920s.
- The song *Yesterday* by the Beatles was first recorded in 1965, and since then it has been 6) .... (record) over 2,000 times by different singers.
- Some rock bands and singers are difficult to please. The band Van Halen used to demand packets of coloured sweets, but with all the brown ones removed because they 7) .... (like) these ones!

GRAMMAR
Past tenses

1 Write sentences. Use the past simple, the past continuous or both.

1 Martha / show / me / her new tablet
    Martha showed me her new tablet.

2 I / not enjoy / the exhibition

3 we / watch / a movie / when / you / phone

4 you / read / that article / about computers / ?

5 I'm sorry, / you / sleep / ?

6 where / you / go / when / I / see/ you / ?

7 I / not pay / for / the software

8 she / work / on her laptop / at the time

2 Choose the correct answers.

1 I *played/playing/was playing* on my computer when suddenly the power went off.

2 My dad asked me to turn down my music because he *watched/watch/was watching* TV.

3 I went into town last weekend and *bought/was buying/buying* a new smartphone.

4 We *tried/were trying/was trying* to find the science museum when Jack remembered that he had Googlemaps on his phone.

5 My cousin *designed/was designing/designing* a new app last year and made quite a lot of money from it.

6 I didn't see my friends last night because I *revised/were revising/was revising* for my exam.

7 Dan *waited/was waiting/were waiting* for us when we arrived at the exhibition.

8 We *decided/were deciding/decide* to go for a walk yesterday while the sun was shining.

3 Complete the text with the correct past simple or past continuous form of these verbs.

decide   form   get   leave   live   return
spend   ~~start~~   study   work

Steve Jobs

Steve Jobs was an American inventor and businessman. He was always interested in technology and 1) _____*started*_____ building computers while he 2) _____ at college. He 3) _____ with his parents at the time. He 4) _____ college after only six months and 5) _____ some time travelling around India. When he 6) _____ to the US, he 7) _____ a job with the technology company Atari. While he 8) _____ there, he 9) _____ to set up his own company. Jobs 10) _____ the Apple company in 1976 with his friend Steve Wozniak, and together they changed the world of phones and personal computing for ever.

4 Choose the correct answers.

1 *Did you use to/You use to/Would you* play football games on the computer when you were younger?

2 We *used watch/would watch/would watching* TV every evening when I was young.

3 I *used to love/would love/use to love* taking photos on my dad's old camera.

4 My grandparents *didn't use to/didn't used to/not use to* have a music player.

5 I *used text/would to text/used to text* my friends every day.

6 My parents *used to live/would live/use to live* in New York.

7 *Did you used to/You use to/Did you use to* buy things online?

8 I *wouldn't have/didn't use to have/not use to have* a mobile phone.

5 Choose the correct answer, A, B or C. Sometimes more than one answer is possible.

1 I _____ in London when I was younger.
  (A) used to live   **B** would live   **(C)** lived
2 I _____ my grandparents every weekend.
  A was visiting   **B** used to visit   **C** would visit
3 Who _____ the mobile phone?
  A invented   **B** used to invent
  C was inventing
4 My grandma _____ scared of technology.
  A was being   **B** used to be   **C** would be
5 It _____ when we left home this morning.
  A used to rain   **B** was raining   **C** raining
6 I _____ my first tablet two years ago.
  A got   **B** was getting   **C** would get
7 I didn't hear my phone last night because I _____.
  A slept   **B** was sleeping
  C used to sleep
8 In the 1980s, most people _____ computers at home.
  A didn't have   **B** didn't use to have
  C wouldn't have

Pronouns

6 Complete the sentences with these reflexive pronouns.

> herself himself ~~myself~~ ourselves
> themselves yourself yourselves

1 I really enjoyed _____ myself _____ at the party.
2 My brother designed the app all by _____ .
3 We paid for the tickets _____ .
4 Did you make this cake _____ , Tom?
5 Mum bought a new computer for _____ .
6 Make sure you all behave _____ while you're out!
7 Dan and Jacob organised the trip _____ .

7 Choose the correct answers.

1 Jane is a friend of *me/my/*(mine.)
2 I love that computer game of *yours/your/you*.
3 Dan showed me a new app of *he's/his/him*.
4 Anna introduced me to a cousin of *her/she/hers*.
5 Are Beth and Sam still working on that project of *their/theirs/they*?
6 We can lend you some books of *our/us/ours*.
7 Have you still got that DVD of *me/mine/my*?

8 Complete the conversations with a reflexive pronoun or *each other*.

A Are you going to the cinema by 1) _____ yourself _____ tonight?
B No, Sam's coming with me. We often go to the cinema with 2) _____ .

A Do George and Milly help 3) _____ with their homework?
B Yes, of course they do! George wouldn't get such good marks if he did all his homework 4) _____ !

A Anna is so selfish! She only thinks about 5) _____ !
B I know. And it's really strange that she and her sister never buy birthday presents for 6) _____ !

A Jack and Fiona are both sitting by 7) _____ on opposite sides of the room.
B Yes, but they keep looking at 8) _____ across the room!

9 Complete the email with one word in each space.

| mailbox | Today | Mail | Calendar | Contacts |

Reply | Reply All | Forward | Delete

To: **Tania**   Subject: **New game!**

Hi Tania,

I wanted to tell you about this new computer game of 1) _____ mine _____ . It's called *Alien Attack.*
I bought it for 2) _____ with my birthday money. It's a game that you can play by 3) _____ , but I think it's more fun if you play with someone else. It was Paul who told me about it. He and his brother play this game with 4) _____ other a lot. He says they can amuse 5) _____ for hours with it.

Why don't you come round this evening? We could order a pizza for 6) _____ , too. I've only got one games controller, but perhaps you could bring one of 7) _____ with you? Let me know what time you can come!

Stella

13

Revision Unit 2

1 **Complete the sentences with these words.**

> access battery charge delete download
> hack program tweet

1 This torch doesn't work. It must need a new
battery .
2 The singer sent a _____ about her next concert.
3 Be careful you don't _____ the file by accident.
4 Only students at the school can _____ this part of the website.
5 I'd love to learn how to _____ a computer to do what I want it to do.
6 Don't forget to _____ your tablet overnight, or you won't be able to use it tomorrow.
7 It only takes a few minutes to _____ a film, and then you can watch it!
8 Someone managed to _____ into my account and steal all my passwords.

2 **Choose the correct answer, A, B, C or D.**

1 Click ____ the 'Go' button to start your search.
  (A) on   **B** to   **C** for   **D** in
2 Key ____ your password and then press 'Enter'.
  A on   **B** in   **C** into   **D** to
3 My computer isn't working. I think it's got a ____ .
  A software **B** code   **C** website **D** virus
4 I can't look at the website now because I haven't got an internet ____ .
  A program **B** software **C** connection **D** online
5 I think you spend too much time in the ____ world of computer games!
  A program   **B** touch screen
  C virtual   **D** website
6 Don't forget to turn ____ your computer before you go to bed.
  A off   **B** down   **C** out   **D** over
7 My brother came up ____ a great idea for a new game.
  A for   **B** in   **C** in   **D** with
8 I keep all my important files in one ____ .
  A code   **B** tweet **C** folder **D** website

3 **Complete the sentences with one word in each space.**

1 I can't work ___out___ the answer to this question.
2 I'll log _____ to my computer and then we can look on the website.
3 Can you zoom _____ and look at our house?
4 It's a really good suggestion, and I'm going to follow it _____ .
5 Scroll _____ to the bottom of the page.

4 **Read the definitions and write the words. Use nouns formed from these verbs.**

> amplify calculate generate instruct
> invent narrate photocopy transmit

1 a machine that can make copies of documents or pictures _photocopier_
2 a machine that makes sounds louder _____
3 a machine that helps you do maths _____
4 a machine that sends out radio signals _____
5 a machine that produces electricity _____
6 someone who tells a story _____
7 someone who teaches you a skill _____
8 someone who thinks of ideas and makes new things _____

5 **Complete the sentences with the correct form of the words in capitals.**

1 My sister wants to be a computer _programmer_ when she leaves school. **PROGRAM**
2 I _____ that man – I really don't think he's honest! **TRUST**
3 She beat all the other _____ in the race. **COMPETE**
4 If you _____ the music player from the speakers, you won't be able to hear any sound. **CONNECT**
5 If the game is still 0–0 at the end, they will have to _____ it next week. **PLAY**
6 IBM is a major _____ in this area. Over 2,000 people work for the company. **EMPLOY**
7 I can use my _____ to send a photo of the document to your computer. **SCAN**
8 I really _____ of young people who behave badly! **APPROVE**

6 Complete the sentences with the correct past simple or past continuous form of these verbs.

> buy   design   do   rain   not try on   ~~walk~~
> watch

1 I met Sara while I _was walking_ home from school.
2 We decided not to play tennis because it
   _____ .
3 I _____ a film when I heard a noise outside.
4 She _____ the shoes before she bought them.
5 My brother _____ an app while he was studying at university.
6 I _____ my homework when my computer crashed.
7 My parents _____ me a new phone because I did very well in my exams last term.

7 Choose the correct answers.

1 My dad (used to live)/used live/would live on a farm.
2 I used to get/getting/was getting very nervous before exams, but I'm OK now.
3 Jack would win/used to winning/won the drama prize last term.
4 My sister would go/used go/was going horse-riding every day when she was younger.
5 I used to have/was having/would have a desktop computer, but I have a tablet now.
6 Did you use to see/Did you used to see/Were you seeing your cousins every weekend?
7 I wasn't/wouldn't/didn't use to like swimming in the sea.

8 Choose the correct answer, A, B or C.

1 I bought ____ a new camera yesterday.
   A me   (B) myself   C mine
2 James lent me an interesting book of ____ .
   A he   B his   C himself
3 I'm going on holiday with a cousin of ____ .
   A me   B mine   C myself
4 My phone is more modern than ____ .
   A your   B yourself   C yours
5 Be careful you don't cut ____ on that knife.
   A you   B yourself   C yours
6 The lights switch ____ on and off while we're out.
   A them   B each other   C themselves
7 Tom's always looking at ____ in the mirror – he's so vain!
   A his   B himself   C each other
8 Toby and Rob often help ____ with homework.
   A theirs   B themselves   C each other

9 Rewrite the sentences using the word given. Use between two and five words, including the word given.

1 No one helped me make this cake.   **ALL**
   I made this cake ____ _all by myself_ ____ .
2 My sister learned to swim by herself.   **TAUGHT**
   My sister _____ swim.
3 They had a good time at the party.   **THEMSELVES**
   They _____ at the party.
4 Sam writes to Kim and Kim writes to Sam. **EACH**
   Sam and Kim _____ .
5 George is my friend.   **OF**
   George is a _____ .
6 Computers were slower in the past.   **USE**
   Computers didn't _____ fast in the past.
7 I started to eat my lunch and then the phone rang. **WHILE**
   The phone rang _____ my lunch.
8 Our old flat wasn't as big as this one.   **USED**
   We _____ in a smaller flat.

10 Complete the blog post with one word in each space.

💬 View previous comments   Cancel   Share   Post

I 1) _was_ talking to my dad about computer games yesterday and he told me about this game – *Pong*. It was one of the first ever computer games. It was a kind of sports game, I think. My dad says it 2) _____ to be quite slow. I don't think it was very exciting! You could play by 3) _____ or two people could play against 4) _____ other. My dad says he and his brother loved it. They 5) _____ play for hours. I'm amazed that they 6) _____ get bored with it!
Anyway, it got me thinking. What other computer games did people 7) _____ to play in the 1970s and 80s? If there are any relatives of 8) _____ who played computer games at this time, I'd love to hear about it!

Write a comment   Support

VOCABULARY

1 Complete the text with nouns formed from these verbs.

achieve ~~experience~~ feel grin hope offer recognise vote

FAME and FORTUNE – is it really worth it?

Contestant Number: 382

Do contestants really enjoy the 1) _experience_ of taking part in TV talent shows? It doesn't always look like it. I guess they feel it's an 2) _____ to get through the auditions to the TV performances, but each week seems to be more painful than the last. You can see the 3) _____ of nervousness that they have before they perform each week. And then, as their 4) _____ of winning the competition fade, you see their desperate appeals to the audience because they know that every 5) _____ counts. What is it that drives them? Is it the desire for 6) _____ of their talents, or perhaps it's that tempting 7) _____ of a recording contract for the winner that encourages them to continue? Whatever it is, surely it can't be worth it, as for every contestant that leaves with a 8) _____ on their face, there are fifty who leave in tears.

2 Choose the correct answer, A, B or C.

1 Tom _____ to help me move flat.
   A felt   B recognised   **C** offered
2 I didn't _____ Sam when I saw him with a beard!
   A recognise   B stare   C experience
3 He finally _____ his goal of becoming a rock singer.
   A felt   B achieved   C voted
4 My hands were _____ because I was so nervous.
   A shaking   B staring   C grinning
5 I really _____ I can get into the final!
   A achieve   B share   C hope
6 People now _____ him by his stage name.
   A experience   B refer to   C vote
7 Thousands of people _____ for her.
   A shared   B experienced   C voted
8 He hates it when people _____ at him.
   A feel   B stare   C share
9 She said she would _____ the prize money with her family.
   A stare   B share   C offer
10 She was _____ because she was so happy.
   A grinning   B achieving   C hoping

3 Unscramble and write the words.

1 Leaving the show was a ___massive___ (sismave) disappointment.
2 I have a real _____ (eessawnk) for chocolate!
3 Her voice is her biggest _____ (trsegthn).
4 It was a great _____ (rliefe) when we knew that everyone was safe.
5 I got an attack of _____ (ernves) before the show.
6 He performed some amazing _____ (fatse) of balance.
7 I felt very _____ (seent) before the final.
8 Everyone was hot and _____ (wsatye).
9 It's important to stay _____ (osptvie).
10 The show had some _____ (nteiagve) reviews.

4 Complete the sentences with these verbs.

crept remained spotted ~~stared~~
vanished waved yelled

1 I couldn't believe what I was seeing, and I just
   _____stared_____ in disbelief at the creature.
2 I _____ quietly out of the door while no
   one was looking.
3 The animal looked at me for a few minutes, and
   then _____ completely!
4 When was the last time someone _____
   the Loch Ness Monster?
5 I called to her, but she _____, 'Go away!'
6 We sat down by the lake and _____ there
   quietly for over two hours.
7 He stood up and _____ goodbye.

5 Complete the tables with these adverbs.

~~carefully~~ eventually frequently happily
here immediately never often outside
quietly there yesterday

Manner		Frequency	
1)	_carefully_	4)	
2)		5)	
3)		6)	

Time		Place	
7)		10)	
8)		11)	
9)		12)	

**6 Put the words in the correct order to make
sentences.**

1 wait / I'll / you / outside / for
   I'll wait for you outside.
2 shouted / us / angrily / at / The man
   _____
3 on TV / never / watch / talent shows / We
   _____
4 call me / immediately / You / if / must /
   happens / anything
   _____
5 Sally / cheerful / always / is
   _____
6 waiting / They / by / were / the bus stop / for us
   _____
7 found / the hotel / We / eventually
   _____

7 Choose the correct answers.

1 The family vanished mystery/
   mysterious/(mysteriously) overnight.
2 Are you lying or are you being truth/truthful/
   truthfully?
3 She walked out onto the stage nerves/nervous/
   nervously.
4 I can't hear anything because of all the noise/
   noisy/noisily.
5 He still felt quite hope/hopeful/hopefully that his
   team could win.
6 The two boys were behaving suspicion/suspicious/
   suspiciously.
7 Jack was feeling really happiness/happy/happily
   that day.
8 He would love to play tennis profession/
   professional/professionally one day.

**8 Complete the text with the correct form of the
words in brackets.**

Teenage heroes steer school bus to safety

Tom Dalton and his friends were chatting
1) _happily_ (happy) on the school bus on their
way home from school last night. Then one of them
2) _____ (sudden) noticed that the driver had
become ill. He had fallen over the wheel and wasn't
steering the bus. Tom and his friends 3) _____
(immediate) ran to the front of the bus. Using all their
4) _____ (strong) they pulled the driver away
from the controls. Tom sat down in the driver's seat and
5) _____ (calm) brought the bus to a stop. At
the same time, Tom's friends looked after the driver and
called an ambulance. Tom says, 'I didn't feel
6) _____ (nerve) at all. I just did what I had to
do. It was a great 7) _____ (feel) when the bus
8) _____ (eventual) stopped moving.' The driver
is still 9) _____ (serious) ill in hospital, but
10) _____ (hope) will make a full recovery.
Meanwhile, Tom and his friends are celebrating
being heroes!

GRAMMAR
Present perfect tenses

1 Put the words in the correct order to make sentences.

1 never / read / book / I / that / have
I have never read that book.

2 been / on TV / has / a few times / She
....

3 been / all morning / have / practising / I
....

4 well / feeling / hasn't / recently / She / been
....

5 a celebrity / met / you / ever / Have / ?
....

6 you / been / What / doing / have / ?
....

7 have / book / I / the worst / ever / It's / read
....

8 first / performed / It's / she / time / the / on stage / has
....
....

9 won / have / a competition / I / never
....
....

2 Choose the correct answers.

1 I've been playing the guitar (for)/since/still ten years.
2 I've called her three times, but she *already/never/still* hasn't called me back.
3 I haven't finished doing my homework *yet/ already/just.*
4 She has wanted to be a singer *for/since/already* she was four years old.
5 Have you *ever/still/yet* sung with a band?
6 Hurry up! The film has *still/already/ever* started!
7 I've known Sara *since/for/yet* about two years.
8 He's applied to be on a few TV shows, but he's *yet/ever/never* been successful.
9 He's *just/still/ever* finished singing, so let's hear what the judges say now.
10 She's the funniest comedian I've *never/ever/still* seen.

3 Complete the conversation with the present perfect simple or present perfect continuous form of the verbs in brackets.

A: We 1) *have been making* (make) a film at school. We started about three months ago but we 2) .... (not finish / yet).

B: How exciting! I 3) ....
(never / be) in a film. Is it difficult to learn all your lines?

A: Yes, I 4) .... (try) to learn them for about six weeks now. I think it's the hardest thing I 5) ....
(ever / do). But I 6) ....
(just / record) all my lines onto my phone, so now I can listen as often as I need to. Hopefully, that will help.

4 Complete the article with the present perfect simple or present perfect continuous form of these verbs.

> already / start ever / happen ~~just / have~~
> reject send tell think try write

Success for young writer

Dale Bradbury is feeling excited. He
1) .... *has just had* .... a letter from a publisher, offering to publish his first novel, *Snowstorm*. Dale, who is only seventeen, 2) ....
to get the novel published for over two years now. He
3) .... the story to more than ten publishers, but until now, all of them
4) .... it. Now he's feeling very positive. 'This is the best thing that
5) .... to me,' he says. 'I
6) .... stories since I was about six years old, but this is the first time that anyone
7) .... me that one of my stories was good enough to publish.' Dale now has plans for the future. He 8) ....
his next novel and he 9) ....
about how he can turn his first story into a film, although he doesn't have any firm plans for that yet.

5 Rewrite the sentences using the word given. Use between two and five words, including the word given.

1 I haven't acted in a play before. **ACTED**
It's the first _____*time I've acted*_____ in a play.

2 I started writing poems two years ago. **WRITING**
I _____ two years.

3 Mike left a few moments ago. **JUST**
Mike _____ .

4 I last saw Sam on Tuesday. **SEEN**
I _____ Tuesday.

5 It started raining five hours ago! **RAINING**
It _____ five hours!

6 It's been three months since I ate meat. **EATEN**
I _____ three months.

7 I've never read such a good book before. **BEST**
This is the _____ read.

Verbs with direct and indirect objects

6 Choose the correct answer, A, B or C.

1 I've bought some flowers _____ .
(A) for you **B** you **C** to you

2 Emma made _____ a cake for my birthday.
A for me **B** me **C** to me

3 He sent an email _____ .
A for me **B** me **C** to me

4 Mrs Adams teaches _____ maths.
A for us **B** us **C** to us

5 I lent _____ some books.
A for Sara **B** Sara **C** to Sara

6 I sold my old bike _____ .
A for Paul **B** Paul **C** to Paul

7 Rewrite the sentences changing the order of the objects (direct or indirect).

1 I've written a letter to the school.
_____*I've written the school a letter.*_____

2 Don't tell this secret to anyone!
_____

3 She read us the letter.
_____

4 My uncle has found me a part-time job.
_____

5 He showed the photos to all his friends.
_____

6 I can send the concert details to you.
_____

8 Complete the email with one word in each space.

mailbox   Today | Mail | Calendar | Contacts

Reply | Reply All | Forward | Delete

To: **Grandma**   Subject: **Thanks!**

Hi Grandma,
Thanks so much for the camera you gave
1) _____*me*_____ for my birthday. I've already taken loads of photos with it. I'll show them
2) _____ you when I see you. Mum and Dad bought some clothes 3) _____ me, which was great, because I never have enough clothes! I got a book from Aunt Sally.
I've promised 4) _____ that I'll read it!
My cards were all lovely. The card from my cousins was really funny – I must send
5) _____ an email to thank them.
I had a really nice day on my birthday. Some of my friends came round and Mum made some food 6) _____ us all. Then I found
7) _____ a DVD to watch, which we all enjoyed.
I'll write again soon and I'll send some more photos
8) _____ you.
Love,
Laura

9 Rewrite the sentences using the word given. Use between two and five words, including the word given.

1 Where did you learn how to ski? **TAUGHT**
Who _____*taught you how*_____ to ski?

2 I borrowed this camera from Matt. **ME**
Matt _____ camera.

3 Who is that text from? **SENT**
Who _____ you?

4 I bought this book from George. **SOLD**
George _____ book.

5 Mike let me see his new tablet. **SHOWED**
Mike _____ tablet.

6 Paul said I could have his old phone. **OFFERED**
Paul _____ me.

7 I got this DVD from my aunt. **GAVE**
My aunt _____ DVD.

Revision Unit 3

1 Complete the words with the missing letters.

1 Going on stage with the band was a great
  e x _p e r i e n c_ e.
2 She's hoping that lots of people will v ___ t ___ for
  her so she wins the show.
3 The men performed some amazing f ___ ___ ___ s
  of strength.
4 I felt horribly hot and s w ___ ___ ___ y after the
  race.
5 I didn't realise that it was Sophie, because she's
  changed beyond r ___ c ___ g n ___ ___ ___ ___ n.
6 I always suffer from n ___ ___ ___ v ___ s before
  important exams.
7 I was upset because my teacher made some
  n ___ g ___ ___ ___ ___ e comments about
  my essay.
8 I could tell she was happy because of the massive
  g ___ ___ n on her face!
9 We've won the Cup – what an
  a ___ ___ ___ ___ v ___ m ___ ___ t!
10 His w ___ k ___ ___ ___ s as a performer is that
  he can't dance very well.

2 Choose the correct answer, A, B or C.

1 We went home ___ an hour.
  A later   B then   **C** after
2 At last ___ big day had arrived!
  A the   B on   C a
3 It only took a ___ of seconds to make my decision.
  A couple   B few   C lot
4 I knew ___ the outset that the trip would
  be a disaster!
  A in   B on   C at
5 I saw him on TV for ___ first time last night.
  A a   B the   C some
6 Sam called me a few minutes ___ .
  A late   B lately   C later
7 She's been busy filming in Europe for the ___
  few months.
  A latest   B last   C recent

3 Match the verbs in the box with the definitions (1–7).

creep remain spot ~~stare~~ vanish
wave yell

1 to look at someone for a long time   _stare_
2 to notice something or someone   _____
3 to stay in a place   _____
4 to disappear   _____
5 to move your hand or arm around
  so that someone will notice you   _____
6 to shout loudly   _____
7 to move in a quiet, careful way   _____

4 Complete the sentences with the correct form of the words in capitals.

1 It took all my ___strength___ to open
  the door.   **STRONG**
2 There was no _____ to the
  accident in the newspaper.   **REFER**
3 It was a really great _____ to
  win the game!   **FEEL**
4 The book gives details of all his
  _____ .   **ACHIEVE**
5 It was such a _____ when we
  finally got home!   **RELIEVE**
6 The children were playing
  _____ outside.   **NOISE**
7 Jack was injured in the accident,
  but _____ he will be OK.   **HOPE**
8 The money vanished _____ .   **MYSTERY**
9 The police arrested her for
  driving _____ .   **DANGER**
10 I'm going to ask you some questions
  and you must answer _____ .   **TRUTH**

5 Complete the sentences with the present perfect simple or present perfect continuous form of these verbs.

> call look rain read sell train
> not try ~~wait~~

1 Why are you so late? We *have been waiting* for hours!
2 *The Hunger Games* is a great novel. I .... it three times!
3 I .... for my passport all afternoon, but I still can't find it!
4 I love Chinese food, but I .... Japanese food yet.
5 I'm really looking forward to running a marathon. I .... for three months now.
6 We .... our car, so now we have to use public transport.
7 Is there something wrong with your phone? I .... you all day and you haven't answered.
8 This weather's so depressing! It .... for five hours!

6 Choose the correct answer, A, B or C.

1 I ..... to the United States.
   A have been never
   B have never been
   C have ever been

2 Have you ..... a unicycle?
   A ever ridden
   B ever been riding
   C ridden already

3 It's OK. I ..... the bill.
   A have already been paying
   B have paid already
   C have already paid

4 Have you ..... ?
   A yet finished eating
   B still finished eating
   C finished eating yet

5 I posted the letter three days ago, but it ..... .
   A still hasn't arrived
   B hasn't already arrived
   C yet hasn't arrived

6 I'm sorry, John isn't here. He ..... .
   A already has left
   B has just left
   C has still left

7 We've been living in London ..... ten years.
   A since   B for   C already

7 Complete the article with one word in each space.

Is this the longest gap year ever?

When Martin Stokes and his girlfriend Anna left university, they decided to take a gap year and go travelling. That was five years ago, and they've 1) ____*been*____ travelling ever since! They have 2) .... been to over twenty countries and they have plans to visit at least ten more before they stop. 'We haven't visited India 3) .... ,' says Anna. 'I really want to go there.' So far, they 4) .... funded their trip by doing casual work when they can. 'Sometimes we work,' says Martin, 'and sometimes people give 5) .... food and shelter for free. People are incredibly kind. Once in the United States we didn't have enough money to buy our train tickets, so someone bought them 6) .... us!' They both agree that this is the best experience they have 7) .... had. 'I know some of our friends 8) .... been working since they left college, but we think this experience is just as valuable as working. Maybe our friends have been earning money 9) .... the last five years, but we've been living!'

8 Rewrite the sentences using the word given. Use between two and five words, including the word given.

1 He started studying English in 2012.   **BEEN**
   He *has been studying* English since 2012.
2 I haven't been to New York before.   **FIRST**
   This is the .... to New York.
3 We moved here six months ago.   **LIVING**
   We .... six months.
4 I haven't eaten nicer food than this.   **EVER**
   This is the .... eaten.
5 Paul bought my old bike from me.   **TO**
   I .... Paul.
6 I received a letter from my aunt.   **SENT**
   My aunt .... letter.
7 My dad said I could have a lift to the station.   **OFFERED**
   My dad .... to the station.
8 Can I borrow your pen?   **LEND**
   Can .... your pen?

VOCABULARY

1 Complete the crossword with words related to money.

```
                    ¹B _ _ _
                     A
 ²   ³               R
 ⁴       ⁵ ⁶         G _ _ _
⁷                   A
                     I
          ⁸ _ _ _ _ N
⁹
     ¹⁰ _ _ _ _ _ _
     ¹¹ _ _ _ _ _ _
```

Across

1 a piece of paper that shows an amount of money you have to pay

5 coins and banknotes

7 someone who buys things in a shop

8 a reduction in the usual price of something

9 a line of people who are waiting for something

10 the whole amount of money that you pay for something (5, 4)

11 a small cart on wheels in which you put things you want to buy in a supermarket

Down

1 something that is good value for money

2 a passage between rows of shelves in a supermarket

3 the place where you pay in a supermarket

4 a piece of paper with a special offer

6 someone who helps you or serves you in a shop

2 Complete the sentences with the correct form of these verbs.

> borrow   cost   economise   ~~lend~~   pay   save   spend   be worth

1 I _____lent_____ John £10 yesterday, and he promised to pay me back today.

2 How much do you _____ on snacks every week?

3 Can I _____ some money to buy a drink?

4 Those shoes look expensive. How much did they _____ ?

5 Some old books _____ a lot of money.

6 I can't come to the cinema with you because I'm trying to _____ .

7 How much does your aunt _____ you for babysitting?

8 You can _____ a lot of money if you buy things online.

3 Choose the correct answers.

1 Jake has got no *common*/*personal* sense at all!

2 Her uncle offered to teach her about *money/personal* finance.

3 If you've got a good level of *common/general* knowledge, why don't you enter our quiz?

4 I'm absolutely hopeless at *money/practical* management – I spend far too much!

5 Are you interested in *higher/common* education after you leave school?

6 It's good to get some *higher/practical* experience of a job while you're still at school.

4 Choose the correct answers.

1 I find it difficult to concentrate *on*/*for/to* my homework if the TV's on.

2 Sara finds it difficult to cope *in/for/with* the stress of exams.

3 Tom has a really good memory *in/for/with* dates.

4 Please pay attention *in/for/to* what I am saying.

5 I've learned the words to the song *at/by/in* heart.

6 You should focus *in/on/to* one thing at a time.

5 Complete the sentences with these words. There are two words which you don't need.

advice attention concentrate cope ~~focus~~
heart help memory

1 I need to _focus_ on improving my maths.
2 Lucy's very quiet. She can't _____ with being in a big crowd of people.
3 I often don't recognise people. I don't have a good _____ for faces.
4 I need a quiet room so I can _____ on writing this essay.
5 Have you ever learned a poem by _____?
6 It's important to pay _____ to the safety demonstration.

6 Complete the study tips with one word from each box.

learning spider ~~study~~ study

diagram methods ~~space~~ style

Tips for successful study

- It's important to have a quiet 1) _study_ _space_ where you can really concentrate on learning.
- Get to know your own individual 2) _____. For example, do you need to see things visually or do you learn better by doing practical things?
- Try out different 3) _____, for example making lists or highlighting words to help you remember them.
- If you're finding it difficult to understand something, it can be useful to draw a 4) _____, to help you understand all the different facts and ideas.

7 Complete the sentences with one word in each space.

1 I hate it when other students mess _about_ in class.
2 If I don't understand a word, I usually _____ it up in an online dictionary.
3 I try to get on _____ my homework as soon as I get home from school.
4 If you don't write _____ what you have to do for homework, you'll forget!
5 We're trying to _____ up a chess club at school.

6 The internet is a great place to find _____ about all kinds of things.

7 I'll be so happy next year, because I can _____ up all the subjects I hate!
8 It's a good idea to look _____ your notes after the lesson, to make sure you understand them all.
9 It's great if you can get _____ by reading about a subject before the lesson.
10 Sometimes when we have to take notes, it can be difficult to _____ up with the teacher, because she talks so fast.

8 Read the blog post and choose the correct answer, A, B or C.

View previous comments   Cancel Share Post

My school diary

Today was a bad day! I got a really bad mark in my history test! I tried to revise, of course, but when I 1) _____ my notes they didn't seem to make any sense! Then in maths the teacher told me off for 2) _____ in class. It really wasn't my fault – honestly! Still, I'm not going to 3) _____ and stop trying. I'm sure I can do better in history if I try to 4) _____ with the teacher in class better and pay more attention to what I 5) _____ . I'm going to make more of an effort in other subjects, too. We're studying volcanoes in geography tomorrow, so I'm going to 6) _____ by trying to 7) _____ about them before the lesson. I'm also trying to 8) _____ a homework club at school. I think I'd find it easier to 9) _____ with my homework if I was in a classroom with no computer games or TV to distract me. Right, I'd better go now and 10) _____ 'volcanoes' online. Should be interesting!

Write a comment   Support

1 A looked up   (B) looked through
   C looked at
2 A finding out   B messing about
   C looking up
3 A give out   B give off   C give up
4 A keep up   B set up   C get ahead
5 A set up   B write down   C give up
6 A set up   B get ahead   C give up
7 A find out   B keep up   C write down
8 A keep up   B set up   C give up
9 A mess about   B find out   C get on
10 A look through   B get on with   C look up

GRAMMAR
Relative clauses

1 Decide if the sentences contain defining (D) or non-defining (N) relative clauses.

1 That restaurant, which opened last year, is very expensive. _N_

2 That's the café where we often have lunch. _____

3 I usually sit next to Tara, who's my best friend. _____

4 Tom, whose father runs his own business, always has loads of money to spend! _____

5 Can you give me back the book that you borrowed last week? _____

6 They found an old picture that's worth over $2,000! _____

2 Choose the correct answers.

1 Jenna was the only person who/which did well in the test.

2 At school, I want to learn about things who/which are important.

3 The library is a quiet place when/where you can read and study.

4 The weekend is a time when/where I relax.

5 That's the coffee shop where/that we often meet for a coffee.

6 Tim is a boy who/whose marks are always good.

7 The programme where/that I watched last night was very interesting.

8 Jack is the friend that/which I spend the most time with.

9 Mia, who/that lives near me, is really interested in cooking.

10 History, that/which is my favourite subject, is easy.

3 Choose the correct answer, A, B or C.

1 Mike, _____ in London, is my best friend.
   A who lives   **B** he lives   **C** who he lives

2 The field _____ we play football is quite close to my home.
   A which   **B** where   **C** that

3 Maria is so spoiled! Her parents buy her everything _____ !
   A who she wants
   B she wants
   C that she wants it

4 That's the girl _____ sister won the lottery!
   A who   **B** who her   **C** whose

5 The internet is a very useful tool _____ help you with your studies.
   A which it can   **B** can   **C** that can

6 Martin, _____ next to me in French, is very good at languages.
   A that sits   **B** who sits
   C where he sits

7 First Aid, _____ about last year, is a useful skill.
   A I learned   **B** that I learned
   C which I learned

4 Join the sentences using the correct relative pronoun in brackets. Use commas only where necessary.

1 This voucher is worth £15. I found it in a magazine. (which / who)
   This voucher, which I found in a magazine, is worth £15.

2 I have an aunt. She loves hunting for bargains. (which / who)
   _____

3 My friend wants to start an online business. Her name is Tina. (who / whose)
   _____

4 I'll take you to the park. I usually meet my friends there. (that / where)
   _____

5 This old radio is now worth £500. I bought it for £20! (which / that)
   _____

6 This film won three Oscars. It cost $20 million. (which / where)
   _____

7 The shoes are lovely. She bought them yesterday. (who / that)
   _____

5 Rewrite the sentences correctly.

1 Simon who wants to be an engineer loves maths.
   Simon, who wants to be an engineer, loves maths.

2 The girl who he met her last week is very nice.

3 Money management, that is a very useful subject, is not taught in schools.

4 That's the discount store who I told you about.

5 This book, I read last year, has lots of interesting information in it.

6 I met someone who brother plays football for Manchester United!

Reduced relative clauses

6 Choose the correct answers.

1 Students *studying*/*studied* philosophy will read works by Aristotle.

2 A lot of the things *sold*/*selling* in that shop are made in China.

3 This is a teaching method *using*/*used* in many parts of the world.

4 Students *living*/*lived* in London find it easier to visit museums and art galleries.

5 The World Cup is a sports competition *watching*/*watched* all over the world.

6 The people *taking*/*took* part in the race come from all over the country.

7 You should take notice of advice *giving*/*given* to you by your teachers.

8 Students *learning*/*learned* languages are often shy about speaking in class.

7 Rewrite the sentences using reduced relative clauses.

1 Italy is a country which is known for its good food.
   Italy is a country known for its good food.

2 Students who are taking the exam should be at school by 8.45.

3 The law which was introduced last year has made no difference.

4 Students who have breakfast before they come to school get better grades.

5 Confucius is a philosopher who is admired all over the world.

6 Supermarkets which offer big discounts are becoming more popular.

7 The subject which was discussed in last week's programme was 'different learning styles'.

8 This is the latest film which features James Bond.

8 Read the article and choose the correct answer, A, B or C.

Maria Montessori

Maria Montessori was an Italian educator 1) _____ a new approach to the education of young children. She grew up in the late nineteenth century, when most of the methods 2) _____ by teachers were very traditional. Teachers stood in front of the class and explained things to children 3) _____ at their desks in rows. Montessori believed that children 4) _____ to discover and learn things on their own, through play, would actually learn more. She opened her first school for young children in 1907. Children 5) _____ the new school were allowed to spend a lot of their time in free play or creative activities. The new kind of education 6) _____ by the school proved extremely popular. Teachers 7) _____ in the school noticed that the children seemed happier and more relaxed than in traditional schools, and they also seemed to learn more. Now there are thousands of Montessori Schools all over the world 8) _____ children according to Maria Montessori's principles.

1 A developing   B developed
   C who developed

2 A using   B they use   C used

3 A sitting   B which were sitting
   C sat

4 A were left   B left   C who left

5 A attended   B who attending   C attending

6 A providing   B provided
   C which provided

7 A worked   B who working   C working

8 A taught   B who taught   C teaching

Revision Unit 4

1 Complete the words with the missing letters.

1 These shoes only cost £15. They were a
   real b _a_ _r_ _g_ _a_ _i_ n!
2 We finished eating and asked for the b ___ ___ l.
3 There were only a few c ___ s ___ ___ ___ ___ s
   in the shop.
4 The shop a ___ ___ s t ___ ___ t helped me find
   the right size.
5 You can pay in c ___ ___ h or by credit card.
6 There's a 10 percent d ___ s ___ ___ ___ ___ t on all
   clothes this week.
7 You'll find tinned foods in the next a ___ s ___ e.
8 Take everything to the c ___ ___ ___ ___ ___ ___ t
   where you can pay for it.
9 My t ___ ___ ___ ___ ___ e y was full of food!
10 There was a long q ___ ___ ___ e of people
   outside the shop.
11 This v ___ ___ ___ ___ ___ r allows you 20 percent
   off fresh fruit and vegetables.
12 The t ___ ___ ___ l c ___ ___ t of the weekly
   grocery shop keeps going up.

2 Choose the correct answers.

1 I'll *pay*/*spend* you £5 if you mend my bike for me.
2 I like your phone. How much did it *cost*/*worth*?
3 I'm *saving*/*economising* money for my holiday.
4 Can I *lend*/*borrow* your pen, please?
5 My mum's ring is *cost*/*worth* nearly £1,000!
6 Could you *lend*/*borrow* me £1 to buy a drink?

3 Complete the sentences with these words.

> by   for   on   on   to   with

1 I want to focus _on_ improving my maths.
2 Have we got to learn all these verbs ___ heart?
3 She never pays attention ___ what the teacher
   is saying!
4 I don't think I can cope ___ all this homework!
5 I can't concentrate ___ my essay when
   everyone's talking!
6 I haven't got a very good memory ___ names.

4 Unscramble and write the words.

1 The answer's obvious – it's just
   common sense ! (mmoonc snsee)
2 You should read more if you want to improve
   your _____ . (gealern nokwedlge)
3 He wants to get a job, rather than go into
   _____ . (herghi cuciondat)
4 Have you got any _____ of working?
   (talpaccir perexceien)
5 My _____ is very visual, so I need to
   see things to learn them well. (lingarne stely)
6 I always draw a _____ to help me
   organise my ideas for an essay. (dipser dramiga)
7 I've got a really nice _____ in my
   bedroom. (sudty pasce)
8 I use a lot of different _____ when
   I'm revising for exams. (syutd mthedso)

**5 Complete the text messages with one word in
each space.**

Messages **Lia**

Hi Anna,
How are you getting 1) _on_ with your
geography homework on fuels? I've looked
2) ___ my notes, but I can't understand
anything! I give 3) ___ !

Hi Lia,
I'm finding it difficult to concentrate 4) ___
homework, too, as it's so warm and sunny
outside. And my little brother's messing 5)
___ with his friends in the next room – that
makes it difficult, to focus 6) ___ work, too!

Well, why don't you come round to my house?
We can see if we can find 7) ___ anything
by looking online, and write 8) ___ the
key points in our books.

Good idea. It's much easier to cope 9) ___
difficult homework when you do it together.
See you soon!

6 Complete the sentences with the correct relative pronouns. Sometimes more than one answer is possible.

1 Here's the DVD ___that___ I was looking for!
2 That's the place _____ I usually sit to have my lunch.
3 The books _____ my grandma used at school were really boring!
4 Mrs Giddings, _____ teaches us French, lived in Paris for three years.
5 1966 was the year _____ England won the World Cup.
6 Physics, _____ is taught in most schools, is quite a difficult subject.
7 Children _____ parents give them a lot of support tend to do better at school.
8 My friend Matt is someone _____ always does well in exams.

7 Choose the correct answer, A, B or C.

1 Sam _____ is very good at tennis.
   A , who lives near me,
   B that lives near me
   C , which lives near me,
2 I've got some photos of the house _____ in France.
   A , where we stay
   B where we stay
   C that we stay
3 The book _____ is about two teenagers from New York.
   A , which I'm reading at the moment,
   B who I'm reading at the moment
   C I'm reading at the moment
4 Sara _____ decided to go home.
   A who was feeling tired
   B was feeling tired
   C , who was feeling tired,
5 My friend Michael _____ has always wanted to study medicine.
   A , who mother is a doctor,
   B , whose mother she is a doctor,
   C , whose mother is a doctor,
6 Mr Simpson is a teacher _____ a lot.
   A , who I admire,
   B that I admire
   C I admire him
7 Her first album _____ sold over a million copies.
   A , it was called *Love alone*,
   B , which was called *Love alone*,
   C , that was called *Love alone*,

8 Complete the reduced relative clauses using the present or past participles of these verbs.

> collect give know ~~study~~ teach wait watch write

1 Students ___studying___ German next year will get the chance to go on a school trip to Germany.
2 The people _____ the film were shocked by some of the violent scenes.
3 The test _____ to the students last term was very difficult.
4 All the money _____ at the charity event will go to help poor children in India.
5 Stephen Hawking is a scientist _____ for his books on the origins of the universe.
6 The books _____ by Charles Dickens in the nineteenth century are still popular today.
7 The people _____ outside the shop are keen to find bargains when the sale starts.
8 The person _____ you history next term will be Mr Sharpe.

9 Rewrite the sentences using the word given. Use between two and five words, including the word given.

1 It's a festival celebrated all over the world. **WHICH**
   It's a festival _which is celebrated_ all over the world.
2 Can you give me back the pen you borrowed last week? **WHICH**
   Can you give me back the pen _____ you last week?
3 Children taught to read before they go to school usually do well. **LEARN**
   Children _____ before they go to school usually do well.
4 Students wanting to come on the trip should add their names to the list. **WANT**
   Students _____ on the trip should add their names to the list.
5 Is there a shop selling souvenirs? **BUY**
   Is there a shop _____ souvenirs?
6 The information you can get on the website isn't always accurate. **GIVEN**
   The information _____ isn't always accurate.

Green world

VOCABULARY

1 Complete the sentences with one word in each space.

1 The country doesn't grow much food, so it is d*ependent* on food from abroad.
2 I prefer to buy o_____ fruit and vegetables because they're grown without chemicals.
3 I always buy r_____ paper because it's better for the environment.
4 They grow most of their own food – they're practically s_____-s_____ .
5 Would you prefer to live in a city or a r_____ area?
6 Destroying the rainforest has a very serious ec_____ impact.
7 Badgers are a p_____ species, which means people aren't allowed to kill them.
8 Foxes can live equally well in the countryside or in an u_____ environment.

2 Complete the sentences with one word from each box.

> be catch ~~die~~ go pick report

> back into on ~~out~~ towards up

1 If we continue to destroy the rainforest, many species will ____*die*____ ____*out*____ .
2 I can't go on the nature walk on Saturday, but Joe's going, and he says he'll _____ _____ and tell me all about it.
3 Our cake sale raised over £150, which will _____ the cost of solar panels.
4 The idea of cycling to school is really starting to _____ , so more and more people are doing it.
5 If you join your local environmental group, you can _____ lots of useful tips about things you can do to make a difference.
6 I don't think I'll ever _____ growing my own food, but I really admire people who do it!

3 Match 1–6 with a–f to make collocations.

1 an urban   a generations
2 a natural   b garden
3 a concrete   c habitat
4 future   d landscape
5 a bus   e jungle
6 a botanical   f route

4 Complete the campaign slogans with these words.

> alternative endangered habitats solar spaces waste

1 Kids need a place to play. Save our public _____*spaces*_____ !

2 Save the whale and other _____ species!

3 No toxic _____ here!

4 Stop destroying wildlife _____ !

5 NO MORE NUCLEAR POWER STATIONS. WE NEED MORE _____ ENERGY!

6 Use _____ panels for green electricity!

5 Read the article and choose the correct answer, A, B, C or D.

Green City

Hamburg in the north of Germany is known for its many factories and 1) _____ . But now the city plans to change its image of being a concrete 2) _____ and become a truly green city. It wants to ban cars from large parts of the city to cut down on traffic 3) _____ and reduce air 4) _____ . Instead, people will be encouraged to cycle on a new Green Network, hundreds of new cycle 5) _____ that are being built all over the city. There will also be improved public 6) _____ to help people move around the city easily. In addition, large parts of the city centre will be for 7) _____ only, making shopping a more pleasant experience. Gina Hoffman from Hamburg is a keen environmental activist. She already has a 8) _____ garden at her flat and is trying to persuade others in her 9) _____ to do the same. She has also campaigned for more 10) _____ bins in the city. She hopes that Hamburg can set an example that other cities can follow.

1	**A** industries	**B**	industrial
	C business	**D**	production
2	**A** forest	**B**	jungle
	C desert	**D**	wood
3	**A** smoke	**B**	dirt
	C steam	**D**	fumes
4	**A** dirt	**B**	smoke
	C pollution	**D**	waste
5	**A** roads	**B**	paths
	C pavements	**D**	walks
6	**A** transport	**B**	travel
	C journey	**D**	voyage
7	**A** walker	**B**	foot
	C pedestrians	**D**	walk
8	**A** ceiling	**B**	top
	C roofed	**D**	rooftop
9	**A** neighbourhood	**B**	neighbours
	C neighbouring	**D**	neighbourly
10	**A** remaking	**B**	reusing
	C recycling	**D**	redoing

(1 **A** industries — circled)

6 Unscramble and write the words related to food and water.

1 In many rural areas, people's only source of drinking water is the village _____well_____ (lelw).

2 People were banned from watering their gardens last summer because there was a _____ (trawe orshaget).

3 After two weeks of rain, there were _____ (fodslo) in many parts of the country.

4 Farmers are being encouraged to use fewer _____ (espictieds) on their crops.

5 No crops will grow in the _____ (dsrtee).

6 There was a _____ (roudght) last summer, with no rain for three months.

7 We collect _____ (anirartew) and use it to water the garden.

8 The country _____ (miorpts) a lot of its food.

9 Organic products are becoming more popular with _____ (csuomenrs).

10 India _____ (eposxrt) tea all over the world.

7 Complete the sentences with one word in each space.

1 I don't understand – it doesn't _____make_____ sense!

2 I always have a cup of coffee in the morning – I really can't do _____ it!

3 We should all _____ our bit to help the environment.

4 _____ sure you switch the lights off before you go out.

5 I'm hot – I could do _____ a drink of water.

6 I can't afford a new car, so I'll have to _____ do with this old one!

8 Read the opinion and choose the correct answer, A, B or C.

I think we should all 1) _____ our bit for the environment. I try to be a responsible 2) _____ and buy things that aren't harmful to the environment. For example, I buy organic fruit because it's grown without 3) _____ . I also try to buy local produce wherever possible, because I think we should aim to reduce the amount the country 4) _____ . It really doesn't make 5) _____ to transport food all over the world!

1	**A** make	**B** do	**C** have
2	**A** producer	**B** consumer	**C** buying
3	**A** pesticides	**B** wells	**C** fumes
4	**A** imports	**B** sells	**C** buys
5	**A** value	**B** sense	**C** logic

(1 **B** do — circled)

GRAMMAR
The future

1 Choose the correct answers.

1 *Are/Do/Will* you meeting Sam this evening?
2 We're *go/going/going to* travel by train.
3 I'm sure you *will/going/going to* have a great time.
4 I can't come to the cinema with you this evening. I'll be *do/doing/going to do* my homework.
5 Where *are/will/do* you going to stay?
6 I'll come and visit as soon *as/that/when* I can.
7 It will be dark by *time/the time/the times* we get home.
8 Where will he be *wait/waits/waiting* for us?

2 Choose the correct answer, A, B or C.

1 I can't talk now, but I _____ you later.
   A call
   B will call
   C am call

2 Do you think it _____ later?
   A will rain
   B is raining
   C going to rain

3 Jane won't be here on Saturday. She _____ on holiday on Friday.
   A will go
   B will be go
   C is going

4 This time next week we _____ on the beach. I can't wait!
   A will lie
   B am going to lie
   C will be lying

5 Dan is going shopping this afternoon. He _____ some new boots.
   A is buying
   B will buying
   C is going to buy

6 I'll text you as soon as I _____ home.
   A get
   B will get
   C am going to get

7 _____ you get this letter, I'll be in New York.
   A By time
   B For the time
   C By the time

8 It's a great film. _____ enjoy it.
   A Definitely you'll
   B You'll definitely
   C You definitely

3 Complete the sentences with the future simple or future continuous form of the verbs in brackets.

1 I'm sure you ___will like___ (like) Tom. He's so nice.
2 I won't be here next week. I _____ (stay) with my aunt in Berlin.
3 If we don't take action, climate change _____ (get) much worse.
4 In three months' time I _____ (study) at university.
5 Give your computer to Ben. He _____ (mend) it for you.
6 The weather _____ (not be) very nice tomorrow.
7 Come round after eight o'clock. I _____ (not revise) then.
8 Is that bag heavy? I _____ (carry) it for you if you like.

4 Rewrite the sentences putting the adverbs in brackets in the correct place.

1 We're going to visit the Louvre. (definitely)
   We're definitely going to visit the Louvre.
2 I'll be revising this evening. (probably)
   _____
3 It will be an interesting experience. (certainly)
   _____
4 She's going to train as a nurse. (possibly)
   _____
5 The meal won't be very expensive. (probably)
   _____

5 Complete the conversation with the correct form of the verbs in brackets.

A What are your plans for the weekend?
B Well, I 1) ___'m going___ (go) shopping with Emily on Saturday morning, but I probably 2) _____ (not buy) anything, because I haven't got any money! Then, when I 3) _____ (get) home I've got loads of revision to do, so I 4) _____ (probably / revise) all afternoon. What about you?
A I 5) _____ (call) Rob to ask him if he wants to get together. He's usually free on Saturday, so we 6) _____ (probably / do) something together. I don't know about Sunday. 7) _____ (you / do) anything exciting on Sunday?
B Not really. Some friends of my parents' 8) _____ (come) over for lunch. By the time they 9) _____ (leave) it 10) _____ (probably / be) quite late. Boring!

so, such, too, enough

6 **Put the words in the correct order to make sentences.**

1 so / dry / It's / that / here / grows / nothing

   It's so dry here that nothing grows.

2 so / people / There / many / were / that / move / you / couldn't

3 see it / It's / film / such / I / want / a / good / that / to / again

4 box / so / The / was / that / heavy / carry it / I / couldn't

5 cold / It's / sit / too / outside / to

6 eat / food / enough / to / There's / everyone / for

7 too / books / carry / There / were / many / for me / to

8 homework / too / I've / much / got / do / to

7 **Choose the correct answer, A, B or C.**

1 I couldn't run _____ keep up with the others.
   A too fast to
   B enough fast to
   C (fast enough to)

2 He's _____ guy that everyone gets on with him.
   A so nice
   B such a nice
   C enough nice

3 She's got _____ money that she doesn't know what to do with it!
   A so much
   B too much
   C so enough

4 There weren't _____ for everyone to sit down.
   A so many seats
   B enough seats
   C too many seats

5 The food was _____ eat.
   A too hot to
   B too much hot to
   C very hot to

6 I was _____ I had to go straight to bed.
   A such tired that
   B tired enough to
   C so tired that

8 **Complete the text with one word in each space.**

Eco Homes

We all know that we waste too 1) _____*much*_____ energy at home and we should cut down. But the fact is that most of the homes we live in just aren't energy-efficient 2) _____ . They use 3) _____ much energy to keep them warm in winter and cool in summer, and that's without all the lighting and modern electrical appliances we all love. Now, more and more people are looking for an eco-home – a home that is comfortable 4) _____ to live in all year round, without using 5) _____ a lot of energy that it damages the environment. This house has 6) _____ solar panels on the roof 7) _____ generate all its own electricity. In fact, last year it generated 8) _____ much electricity that it sold some to the main electricity supplier. Owner Adam Trilby is delighted with his eco-house. 'It's good to know we're helping the environment,' he says, 'and it's 9) _____ a cheap house to live in that we now have more money to spend on other things.'

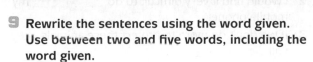

9 **Rewrite the sentences using the word given. Use between two and five words, including the word given.**

1 It was so hot that we couldn't play tennis. **TOO**
   It was _____*too hot to play*_____ tennis.

2 The water was too cold to swim in. **ENOUGH**
   The water _____ swim in.

3 It rained such a lot that the river flooded. **SO**
   There was _____ the river flooded.

4 There were so many birds that you couldn't count them. **MANY**
   There were _____ count.

5 The dress was so expensive that I decided not to buy it. **SUCH**
   It was _____ I decided not to buy it.

6 He invited so many people that they couldn't all get into the house! **LOT**
   He invited _____ people that they couldn't all get into the house!

Revision Unit 5

1 Complete the sentences with the correct form of the words in capitals.

1 The oil spill caused an _____ecological_____ disaster. **ECOLOGY**

2 Many people believe that we are too _____ on oil and fossil fuels. **DEPEND**

3 We should try to preserve the natural world for future _____ . **GENERATE**

4 Tigers are an _____ species. **DANGER**

5 There is too much air _____ in our cities. **POLLUTE**

6 We need more _____ bins in the city. **RECYCLE**

7 This is a very pleasant _____ to live in. **NEIGHBOUR**

8 You aren't allowed to camp here, as it's a _____ area. **PROTECT**

2 Complete the sentences with one word in each space.

1 I don't really want a big garden because I'm not _____into_____ gardening.

2 I would find it very difficult to do _____ my mobile phone.

3 If we don't do more to protect these animals, they will die _____ .

4 This money will go _____ providing clean water in rural areas.

5 This is the only food we've got, so we'll have to make do _____ it.

6 Do you think that solar-powered phones will ever catch _____ ?

7 We went to a green living exhibition to pick _____ some ideas.

8 Mike went to the talk and then reported _____ to us.

3 Complete the sentences with these words.

> botanical concrete fumes ~~national~~
> natural rooftop route shortage

1 The area is a _____national_____ park, so it's protected.

2 She's into _____ gardening and has lots of plants up there, as well as a fantastic view!

3 We saw some wonderful plants in the _____ garden.

4 As far as I'm concerned, the city is a _____ jungle and I'd hate to live there!

5 There was a severe water _____ last summer.

6 I can't stand the smell of traffic _____ !

7 This woodland area is an important _____ habitat for plants and animals.

8 Which bus _____ is your home on?

4 Complete the sentences with one word in each space.

1 A city is an u_____rban_____ environment.

2 If people are s_____-s_____ , they produce all the food that they need to eat.

3 Public s_____ are areas in a town or city where people can go to spend time or relax.

4 T_____ waste is waste material that is dangerous and harmful to people's health.

5 P_____ are people who are walking in a town or city.

6 If the roads and fields are covered in water, they are f_____ .

7 When a country e_____ goods, it sells them to another country.

8 A d_____ is a very dry area where few plants grow.

9 A d_____ is a long period of time without rain.

10 A w_____ is a hole in, the ground from which people get water.

5 Choose the correct answers.

GOING GREEN
WHAT CAN YOU DO?

- Try to become a green 1) (consumer/user/transport) and only buy things that are environmentally-friendly.
- Don't drive places, but use public 2) export/import/transport instead, or think about cycling to school or work. There are plenty of cycle 3) roads/paths/pavements in most cities.
- Encourage your school or place of work to invest in 4) alternative/recycling/waste energy technology such as solar 5) panels/paths/spaces.
- Buy 6) nature/organic/chemical foods wherever possible, to cut down on the use of 7) rainwater/pesticides/pollution.
- Campaign to preserve wildlife 8) habits/habitats/spaces to help endangered 9) species/waste/desert.

6 Put the words in the correct order to make sentences.

1 tomorrow / time / I'll / This / skiing / be

   This time tomorrow I'll be skiing.

2 going / Where / to have / lunch / we / are / ?

   _____

3 definitely / rain / It's / going / to / later

   _____

4 next / time / travelling / year / I'll / This / be /

   _____

5 probably / late / The train / be / will

   _____

6 need / an umbrella / won't / We / definitely

   _____

7 Complete the sentences with one word in each space.

1 What are you ___going___ to do in the holidays?

2 Do you think that polar bears _____ die out when all the ice melts?

3 I'm quite tired, so I probably _____ go out.

4 What _____ you doing on Sunday?

5 My grandma will _____ sitting by the fire, as usual!

6 Where _____ you be living next year?

7 I'm _____ going to learn to drive yet – it's too expensive!

8 I'll come as soon _____ I can.

9 It will open in three months' _____ .

10 Dinner will be ready _____ the time you get home.

8 Choose the correct answers.

1 The soup was (so)/such hot that I couldn't eat it.

2 There isn't enough/so much land to grow all the food we need.

3 She's so/such a popular girl that everyone invites her to their parties.

4 The issue of climate change is so/too important to ignore.

5 The weather was so/such bad that we couldn't go out.

6 Do you think there's so much/too much violence on TV?

7 The bag isn't enough big/big enough to take everything.

8 I've got such a lot/so lots of books that I need some more shelves.

9 Sara spends so much/such a lot time working that she never enjoys herself!

10 You shouldn't eat too much/too many sweets.

9 Rewrite the sentences using the word given. Use between two and five words, including the word given.

1 The film was too boring to watch! **SO**
   The film was ___so boring that I___ couldn't watch it.

2 My parents think I'm too young to go on holiday alone. **ENOUGH**
   My parents think I _____ go on holiday alone.

3 Mia's got so many clothes that they won't all fit in her wardrobe. **LOT**
   Mia's got _____ that they won't all fit in her wardrobe.

4 I didn't work very hard, so I didn't pass my exam. **ENOUGH**
   I didn't _____ my exam.

5 The book was so good that I recommended it to all my friends. **SUCH**
   It was _____ I recommended it to all my friends.

6 There were such a lot of people that they didn't all fit on the boat. **TOO**
   There were _____ fit on the boat.

Before time

VOCABULARY

1 Complete the sentences with these words.

> breath dry face goose-bumps heart
> lump nerves ~~pale~~ shivers sigh

1 Her face went _____pale_____ when she saw the huge creature.
2 We all breathed a _____ of relief when we realised that there was nothing there.
3 My mouth went _____ and I could hardly speak.
4 I took a deep _____ and slowly opened the door.
5 We all had _____ on our skin from standing outside in the cold.
6 My _____ began to thump with fear.
7 I suddenly heard a loud roar which sent _____ down my spine.
8 I don't know what I would do if I came face-to-_____ with a wild animal.
9 The noise of the machines was beginning to get on my _____ .
10 It was sad when they left and I had a _____ in my throat as I said goodbye.

2 Look at the picture and write the words.

> back elbow knee neck shoulders

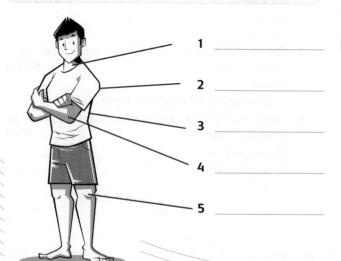

1 _____
2 _____
3 _____
4 _____
5 _____

3 Complete the puzzle and find the mystery word.

1 L	U	N	G	S
		2		
		3		
4				
			E	
		5		
		6		
7				

1 the part of your body where air goes when you breathe it in
2 the bone around your head
3 the part of your body that pumps blood around your body
4 the strong parts of your body that help you to move your arms and legs
5 the part of your body where food goes when you eat it
6 the hard parts inside your body that give it strength
7 the part of your body in your head that you use for thinking

Mystery word: _____

4 Complete the sentences with these words.

> ~~claws~~ fur skin tail wings

1 Some animals use their sharp _____claws_____ to kill other animals.
2 Birds can fly because they have _____ .
3 Cats have very soft _____ .
4 Your _____ covers your whole body.
5 A crocodile has a long _____ .

5 Read the article and choose the correct answer, A, B, C or D.

The oldest humans in Europe

In 2014 scientists came 1) _____ what looked like ancient human footprints in rocks on the east coast of Britain. They weren't able to 2) _____ up any equipment or dig the footprints 3) _____ in order to preserve them, because they knew the tide would come back in and wash them away. But they had time to study them and work 4) _____ their age. It seems the prints date 5) _____ to 850,000 years ago, making them the oldest humans in Europe. Far older prints have been found from Africa, but these prints help scientists to understand when our ancestors first 6) _____ out from Africa for Europe. They have pointed 7) _____ that this discovery leads them to believe this event was earlier than previously thought. No one has yet come up 8) _____ an explanation for why these footprints are there, but scientists will 9) _____ on studying finds such as these in an effort to understand the history of early humans.

1	**(A)** across	**B** up	**C** with	**D** for
2	**A** get	**B** set	**C** make	**D** let
3	**A** in	**B** away	**C** up	**D** down
4	**A** up	**B** out	**C** away	**D** in
5	**A** away	**B** from	**C** back	**D** up
6	**A** set	**B** got	**C** let	**D** made
7	**A** up	**B** for	**C** to	**D** out
8	**A** to	**B** for	**C** with	**D** at
9	**A** keep	**B** get	**C** make	**D** do

6 Match the adjectives (1–9) with the strong adjectives (a–i) with a similar meaning.

1	tired	**a**	terrifying
2	bad	**b**	enormous
3	big	**c**	marvellous
4	nice	**d**	deafening
5	dirty	**e**	exhausted
6	full of people	**f**	horrified
7	loud	**g**	dreadful
8	frightening	**h**	filthy
9	upset	**i**	packed

7 Complete the adjectives with the missing letters.

1 Lucy is an _a_ m _a_ _z_ _i_ n g football player.
2 This g _____ n t lizard is the biggest in the world.
3 That was an a _____ s _____ m e film – I loved it!
4 We couldn't go out because the weather was so a _____ _____ _____ l.
5 Oh, no. This is t _____ _____ b _____ news!
6 I took a bite of the meat, but it tasted h _____ r _____ b _____ .

8 Complete the sentences with these words.

1 Our clothes soon dried in the _____baking_____ heat.
2 The piano is quite a modern _____ instrument.
3 Do you think it is important to learn about _____ civilisations?
4 We visited some famous _____ sites from the nineteenth century.
5 There was a terrible storm, with _____ rain.

9 Complete the text with the correct form of the words in brackets.

The Moai

When European travellers first visited Easter Island in the South Pacific Ocean, they were 1) __amazed__ (amaze) to find a collection of large stone statues. At first, no one knew who had made the 2) _____ (mystery) statues. They now know that the 887 statues, called Moai, were made by the Rapa Nui people. The statues were probably carved between 1250 and 1500, but the Rapa Nui have a culture of considerable 3) _____ (sophisticated) which dates back to the first millennium AD.

The statues are carved in quite a plain style, with very little 4) _____ (decorate). Some of the statues have 5) _____ (colour) red headdresses, which experts believe were a sign of power or wealth.

Historians believe that creating and moving the statues must have been quite a 6) _____ (complicate) business, involving a large number of people.

Visitors to the island have always been 7) _____ (fascinate) by the statues and in 1995 campaigners were 8) _____ (succeed) in gaining recognition for the statues, as they were declared a world heritage site.

GRAMMAR
Past perfect simple

1 Complete the sentences with the past perfect simple form of these verbs.

> forget give ~~leave~~ not organise see
> not tidy visit

1 I couldn't buy a ticket because I ___had left___ my money at home.
2 My mum was angry because I _____ my room.
3 Jenny was upset about losing her watch because her grandmother _____ it to her.
4 I didn't go to the cinema with my friends because I _____ the film before.
5 I went to New York last summer, and that was the first time I _____ the United States.
6 The trip didn't go well because we _____ it carefully enough.
7 My phone ran out of battery because I _____ to charge it the night before.

2 Choose the correct answer, A, B or C.

1 I didn't order any food because I _____ .
   A had before eaten
   B had already eaten ⓑ
   C already eaten
2 The train _____ when I got to the station.
   A had just left
   B already had left
   C had left before
3 They had been friends _____ five years old.
   A since they were
   B since they had been
   C already they were
4 Tom was excited _____ a competition.
   A before he had won
   B because he had won
   C because he already won
5 I realised when I started reading the book that I _____ .
   A read it before
   B had read it before
   C had read it just
6 Scientists had studied the creatures _____ before they made this important discovery.
   A since many years
   B for many years
   C already many years

3 Complete the second sentence with the past simple or the past perfect simple.

1 I ate my lunch and then I called Matt.
   I called Matt when I ___had eaten___ my lunch.
2 I lost my purse, so I didn't have any money.
   I didn't have any money because I _____ my purse.
3 Gina arrived and I made some coffee.
   When Gina _____ , I made some coffee.
4 I failed my exam and I felt really upset.
   I felt really upset when I _____ my exam.
5 They paid their bill and then they left the hotel.
   They left the hotel when they _____ their bill.
6 I asked Tom to come with us and he agreed.
   When I _____ Tom to come with us, he agreed.
7 Last summer, scientists found some dinosaur bones here for the first time.
   It was the first time scientists _____ dinosaur bones here.
8 I spent all my money and then I went home.
   I went home when I _____ all my money.

4 Complete the text with the correct form of the verbs in brackets.

What killed the dinosaurs?

In the past, scientists believed that the dinosaurs 1) ___died___ (die) out when a giant meteor from outer space 2) _____ (hit) the earth around 66 million years ago. At that time, dinosaurs 3) _____ (live) on the earth for millions of years. According to the theory, the meteor 4) _____ (cause) a massive explosion, which 5) _____ (lead) to a period of darkness. This lack of sunlight 6) _____ (kill) all the plants that dinosaurs 7) _____ (eat) for thousands of years. However, some scientists now believe that when the meteor struck, dinosaurs 8) _____ (already / start) to struggle for survival. It seems that a series of volcanic eruptions 9) _____ (already / cause) problems for these giant creatures, by changing the climate and making it hard for them to find food. Scientists now believe that the explosion caused by the meteor 10) _____ (be) simply the final, fatal blow to these magnificent animals.

Comparatives and superlatives

5 Put the words in the correct order to make sentences.

1 smaller / The room / remembered / than / was / had / I

   The room was smaller than I had remembered.

2 work / didn't / Cara / as / quickly / as me

3 difficult / This exam / more / than / the last one / was

4 the world / oldest / bones / These / in / are / the

5 The exhibition / as popular / expected / wasn't / we / as / had

6 most / This / about / dinosaurs / is / the / surprising thing

7 My sister / less / interested / is / in / history / me / than

8 Jack / run / as me / can't / fast / as

6 Rewrite the sentences using the words in brackets.

1 The tickets don't cost as much as last year. (less)
   The tickets _are less expensive than_ last year.

2 The park wasn't as close as we thought. (than)
   The park _____ we thought.

3 Jack did much better than me in the test. (as)
   I didn't _____ Jack in the test.

4 I find French much easier than Spanish. (far)
   I find Spanish _____ French.

5 No other historical site in the world is as important as this one. (the)
   This is _____ site in the world.

6 Lia is a much quicker learner than I am. (quickly)
   Lia _____ I do.

7 The bridge isn't quite as ancient as the tower. (less)
   The bridge _____ the tower.

8 I didn't set off quite as late as the others. (bit)
   I set off _____ the others.

7 Read the article and choose the correct answer, A, B or C.

The ancient Roman city of Pompeii is one of 1) _____ important historical sites in the world. Although the city wasn't 2) _____ as the capital, Rome, it was still a lively bustling city. But 3) _____ remarkable thing about Pompeii is the way in which it was destroyed. In AD 79 a volcanic eruption, that was 4) _____ powerful than any of more recent times, buried the city within a few days. Because Pompeii was destroyed so quickly, it is one of 5) _____ preserved cities from the time of ancient Rome. Most historical sites such as palaces and temples tell us a lot about how the rich and powerful lived. Pompeii can tell us about how ordinary people, including 6) _____ people in society, lived. It gives us 7) _____ idea of what everyday life was like than many other sites. For example, food preserved on street stalls can show us that ordinary people had a 8) _____ varied diet than we might expect. Without the destruction of Pompeii in AD 79, we wouldn't be nearly 9) _____ informed about life in the ancient Roman empire as we are.

1 A most	**B** the most	**C** the more
2 A bigger		
B slightly as big		
C nearly as big		
3 A the more	**B** more	**C** the most
4 A much more	**B** lot more	**C** bit more
5 A the most perfect		
B the most perfectly		
C more perfectly		
6 A poorest	**B** the poorer	**C** the poorest
7 A the much best		
B the much better		
C a much better		
8 A far	**B** far more	**C** far most
9 A well	**B** better	**C** as well

Revision Unit 6

1 Choose the correct answers.

1 We all breathed a sigh of *pale/nerves/relief* when we saw that she was safe.

2 I had a lump in my *throat/mouth/tongue* at the end of the film.

3 The horrible sound sent *shivers/fears/shakes* down my spine.

4 My heart was *hitting/thumping/slapping*, I was so scared.

5 His constant whistling really *gets/goes/gives* on my nerves!

6 What time are you setting *in/out/away* tomorrow?

7 Have you *worked/taken/went* out the answer yet?

8 They *got/went/came* across some ancient remains in Spain last year.

9 He came *out for/up with/over to* some good ideas.

10 I think we should *come on/get on/keep on* searching for bones.

2 Complete the text with these words.

> bones brain claws elbow muscles neck
> skeletons skin skull ~~tail~~

Tyrannosaurus rex was the largest of all dinosaurs, measuring over 12 metres from its nose to the tip of its 1) _____*tail*_____ . Scientists have been lucky enough to find several complete 2) _____ of this amazing creature and so have been able to study it in some detail. We know that its head was massive because the largest 3) _____ that has been found measures 1.5 metres. T. rex had a thick, strong 4) _____ to support its huge head. Its front legs were quite short, with an 5) _____ in the middle which could bend. At the end of its front legs were extremely powerful 6) _____ , which it used for catching and killing smaller dinosaurs.

Its back legs were large and had huge, powerful 7) _____ , which helped it to run fast. Although T. rex looks very heavy, in fact the huge 8) _____ in its legs were hollow, which kept its weight down and allowed it to run faster. We obviously don't know what colour 9) _____ T. rex had, but scientists believe it was probably brown or dark green, like that of a modern crocodile. Although T. rex had a huge head, the 10) _____ inside its head was relatively small, so unfortunately it wasn't the smartest of animals!

3 Unscramble and write the words in the correct column.

> ~~sasmvie~~ readdluf nowredluf iagnt fulwa
> nafsattic guhe retrbile ramlevlsou

bad	nice	big
1) _____	4) _____	7) _*massive*_
2) _____	5) _____	8) _____
3) _____	6) _____	9) _____

4 Complete the sentences with one word in each space.

1 Do you play any m_____*usica*_____l instruments?

2 We visited some interesting h_____l sites.

3 We couldn't walk for long in the b_____g heat.

4 Do you think it's important to study a_____t civilisations?

5 It's sunny now, but there was t_____l rain earlier!

5 Complete the sentences with the correct form of the words in capitals.

1 She refused to eat the food because it was so _*disgusting*_ . **DISGUST**

2 I was _____ to see how much the place had changed. **AMAZE**

3 I applied to get onto the show, but I didn't have any _____ . **SUCCEED**

4 This film is really good _____ for the whole family. **ENTERTAIN**

5 No one can explain his _____ disappearance. **MYSTERY**

6 I think we should put up a few _____ to make the room look nice. **DECORATE**

7 I've always been _____ by the natural world. **FASCINATE**

8 I think her designs are too simple and lack _____ . **SOPHISTICATED**

6 Choose the correct answers.

1 The film *started/had started* when I *got/had got* to the cinema, so I missed the first ten minutes.

2 When I *met/had met* George, he *told/had told* me all about his problems.

3 Finally, we *arrived/had arrived* home and *were/had been* able to relax.

4 When I *went/had been* to Africa last year, it was the first time I *saw/had seen* elephants in the wild.

5 We *weren't/hadn't been* hungry in the evening because we *ate/had eaten* such a big lunch.

6 Sara *showed/had shown* me some photos which she *took/had taken* on holiday in Austria.

7 Lots of people *came/had come* to my party and they all *gave/had given* me presents.

8 I was delighted when I *discovered/had discovered* that I *won/had won* the competition.

7 Cross out one unnecessary word in each sentence.

1 We had known each other for since ten years.

2 I tried calling Sam yesterday morning, but he just had already left for school.

3 It was really exciting going to Brazil because we hadn't been already to South America before.

4 Max had gone just home because he was tired.

5 We had been there for since ten o'clock.

6 The concert had already started when I had got to the theatre.

7 It was the best film I already had ever seen.

8 When Jonathan called, we already had just finished eating.

8 Rewrite the sentences using the word given. Use between two and five words, including the word given.

1 I hadn't spoken to Mark before yesterday.   **FIRST**
Yesterday was the *first time I had spoken* to Mark.

2 Julia left before we arrived.   **ALREADY**
Julia _____ when we arrived.

3 The train left a short time before we got to the station.   **JUST**
The train _____ when we got to the station.

4 I was in Paris for the first time.   **BEFORE**
I hadn't _____ .

5 I had first met Jack when I was fifteen.   **SINCE**
I _____ I was fifteen.

9 Complete the sentences with the correct form of the words in brackets. Add extra words if necessary.

1 I think the ancient Greek civilisation is _____*more interesting than*_____ (interesting) the ancient Egyptian one.

2 Who do you think is _____ (good) singer in the world?

3 You need to work _____ (hard) this if you want to pass your exams!

4 Dan isn't _____ (clever) as he thinks he is!

5 My mum is one of _____ (patient) people I know.

6 That's _____ (bad) film I've ever watched!

7 Cara can work _____ (quickly) than anyone else I know.

8 The weather today isn't _____ (good) as it was yesterday.

10 Rewrite the sentences using the word given. Use between two and five words, including the word given.

1 Paul isn't quite as intelligent as his brother.   **SLIGHTLY**
Paul is *slightly less intelligent than* his brother.

2 Gold coins are slightly more valuable than bronze ones.   **AS**
Bronze coins _____ as gold ones.

3 Leather shoes cost a lot more than canvas ones.   **MUCH**
Leather shoes are _____ canvas ones.

4 The monument wasn't nearly as big as I expected.   **FAR**
The monument _____ I expected.

5 Sara isn't as competitive as her sister.   **LESS**
Sara _____ her sister.

6 The site is slightly more popular now.   **BIT**
The site _____ now.

VOCABULARY

1 Complete the sentences with one word in each space.

1 C*ompetitors* are people who are taking part in a sport or competition.

2 Your o_____ are the people you are against in a sport or competition.

3 A c_____ is someone who teaches people how to do a sport.

4 Your p_____ g_____ is all the people you know who are the same age as you.

5 Your m_____ are your friends.

6 A school c_____ is a group of teachers and students who help to make decisions about the school.

2 Choose the correct answers.

1 Do you want to *take/have/get* part in the race next week?

2 Oh, no. I think I've *done/made/got* a silly mistake!

3 My brother started studying medicine, but he didn't like it so he changed *way/path/direction* and now he's doing law.

4 We walked all day and then *put out/got at/set up* camp near a river in the evening.

5 We couldn't *find/get/see* our way in the dark.

6 I hope I'll be able to *stand/run/walk* on my own two feet when I'm eighteen.

7 It doesn't taste very nice at the moment, but a little more salt should do the *task/trick/difference*.

3 Complete the article with one word in each space.

Is life getting you 1) ___*down*___ ? We all feel depressed sometimes but don't worry – we've got lots of ideas to help cheer you 2) _____ .

• Go on a short holiday. We all need to get 3) _____ from home from time to time and when you get 4) _____ , you'll probably feel much better.

• Take up a new hobby. You might not feel very keen at first, but if you can find something you're interested in, it will gradually draw you 5) _____ , and you'll forget that you were ever depressed.

Good luck!

4 Choose the correct answer, A, B or C.

1 I'm absolutely hopeless _____ tennis!
   A for   B of   C at ✓

2 My brother is hooked _____ computer games!
   A on   B at   C in

3 A lot of people are afraid _____ spiders.
   A for   B off   C of

4 I don't think you should be embarrassed _____ your appearance.
   A for   B at   C about

5 Jen is very popular _____ everyone at school.
   A with   B among   C for

6 I love it when my parents say that they are proud _____ me!
   A at   B for   C of

5 Complete the blog post with one word in each space.

View previous comments   Cancel   Share   Post

I was having a tough time at school last year. Problems with friends were getting me 1) ___*down*___ , so I started spending more and more time online. It was my way of getting 2) _____ from my problems, I guess, but after a few months I realised that I was completely addicted 3) _____ social media. It ruled my life! I didn't take part 4) _____ any activities at the weekend because I was worried 5) _____ missing an important chat with my online friends. I decided I needed to become more confident and learn to stand on my 6) _____ two feet. So I joined a local choir. I never thought I was brilliant 7) _____ singing and I was a bit anxious 8) _____ singing in front of other people. But it turns out that I've got quite a good voice. Now I'm really passionate 9) _____ singing. Even if I'm feeling a bit down, singing always cheers me 10) _____ . Why don't you give it a go?

Write a comment   Support

6 Find eight adjectives to describe people. The words go across, down or diagonally. The first letter of each word is highlighted.

i	p	r	c	o	n	f	i	d	e	n	t
n	m	c	a	i	a	r	m	i	d	o	r
c	r	a	r	e	m	n	i	e	r	t	i
r	i	u	g	h	b	i	x	p	r	o	w
e	a	t	i	i	u	s	l	i	p	s	l
a	n	i	l	n	n	t	a	w	o	n	o
t	r	o	p	r	o	a	r	e	a	u	u
i	l	u	a	m	b	i	t	i	o	u	s
v	o	s	n	o	l	p	m	i	c	s	p
e	a	t	s	p	a	c	t	i	v	e	r
s	p	r	o	t	e	c	t	i	v	e	o

7 Complete the sentences with these adjectives.

active ~~adventurous~~ aggressive ambitious competitive creative decisive protective self-sufficient supportive

1 My brother loves doing new and exciting things. He's very _adventurous_ .
2 I find it very difficult to make decisions about what to do. I'm not very _____ .
3 I definitely want to do well in life, so I guess I'm _____ .
4 My friends were all very _____ and helped me a lot last year when I was having problems.
5 I hate sitting around doing nothing. I prefer to be _____ !
6 My sister doesn't seem to need other people at all. She's completely _____ .
7 Leah doesn't care if she wins or loses games. She's not _____ at all.
8 My parents worry about me too much and they never want to let me do anything. I think they're too _____ of me.
9 I really don't like people who lose their temper and shout at others. There's no need to be _____ like that!
10 Anna is always making beautiful things. She's very _____ .

8 Choose the correct answers.

1 Sailing is quite a *danger/dangers/dangerous* sport.
2 I was beginning to *suspect/suspicious/suspicion* that Marty was the thief.
3 The high winds during the storm were very *destroy/destruction/destructive*.
4 My parents would be *fury/furious/furiously* if I failed all my exams.
5 Do you think that most teenagers *depend/depends/dependent* on their phones too much?
6 I'm really not interested in *fame/famously/famous* or wealth.
7 I think Lisa is a very *attract/attractive/attraction* person.
8 It's good to have lots of *differ/differs/different* hobbies, I think.

9 Complete the advert with the correct form of the words in brackets.

Circus skills for teenagers

Would you like to try something 1) _adventurous_ (adventure) this summer? If you are young and 2) _____ (act) and enjoy learning new skills, why not try one of our circus skills courses? Our 3) _____ (support) coaches will train you in all the main circus skills like juggling and riding a unicycle. And don't worry – although some of the activities look a bit 4) _____ (danger), we'll make sure you wear 5) _____ (protect) clothing so that if you fall you won't hurt yourself. Doing one of our courses will increase your 6) _____ (confide) and make you less 7) _____ (caution) about trying new things. So, if you have a 8) _____ (suspect) that you could be our next big star, go to our website at www.circusadventure.co.uk and sign up now!

GRAMMAR
Modal verbs (1)

1 **Choose the correct answers.**

1 You spend too much time on your computer. You (should)/can't spend more time outdoors.

2 My parents were very strict when I was younger, so I can't/couldn't stay out late.

3 The bus leaves at nine, so we mustn't/don't need to be late.

4 Tom is great at scoring goals, but he can't/couldn't run very fast.

5 Must/Would you pass me the salt, please?

6 Thanks for the invitation, but I shouldn't/had better ask my parents before I say yes.

7 Do you think you were allowed/will be allowed to come with us next Saturday?

8 We have to/needn't worry about food, because my mum says she'll buy us pizzas.

9 My sister can/was able to swim when she was only three years old.

10 May/Should I open the window, please? I feel a bit faint and I need some fresh air.

2 **Complete the email with one word in each space.**

mailbox   Today | Mail | Calendar | Contacts

Reply | Reply All | Forward | Delete

To: **Tara**   Subject: **Ice skating?**

Hi Tara,
Do you think you 1) _____will_____ be allowed to come ice skating with me on Saturday? You don't need 2) _____ worry about paying because my mum is paying for everything. It's my birthday treat! You must wear gloves, but you 3) _____ have to take your own skates – you can hire them there. I hope I'll 4) _____ able to stay on my feet this time. The last time I went skating, all I 5) _____ do was move around the edge, holding on! Anyway, I 6) _____ better get on with my homework now.
I've 7) _____ to finish my geography project. See you on Saturday – I hope!
Mia

3 **Read the conversations and choose the correct answer, A, B or C.**

Stephan	1) _____ I go home early today? I 2) _____ finish an essay tonight.	
Coach	Yes, that's OK, but you 3) _____ be more organised in future. You 4) _____ to play in the team if you keep missing training.	
Cara	5) _____ I go to Jo's party on Saturday?	
Mum	I'm not sure. Grandma's coming to visit, so you 6) _____ to spend some time with her.	
Cara	I know, but it's not fair. All my friends 7) _____ to go. I'll be the only one who misses it!	
Mum	Well, I guess it will be OK. But you 8) _____ make sure that you do all your homework on Saturday, before you go.	
Cara	Great. Thanks, Mum. Oh, and 9) _____ you wash my jeans for me, please? I want to wear them on Saturday.	

1 **A** Would   (B) May   **C** Must
2 **A** have got   **B** mustn't   **C** need to
3 **A** must   **B** have got   **C** ought
4 **A** can't   **B** shouldn't **C** won't be able
5 **A** Can   **B** Must   **C** Should
6 **A** should   **B** better   **C** ought
7 **A** were allowed
  B can
  C will be allowed
8 **A** needn't   **B** had better **C** ought
9 **A** should   **B** can't   **C** would

4 **Rewrite the sentences using the word given. Use between two and five words, including the word given.**

1 The teachers say we can't use our phones in class.   **ALLOWED**
We _____aren't allowed to use_____ our phones in class.

2 Maria shouldn't work so hard!   **OUGHT**
Maria _____ so hard!

3 It won't be possible for me to come with you.   **ABLE**
I _____ come with you.

4 It isn't necessary to buy a ticket in advance.   **HAVE**
You _____ a ticket in advance.

5 You shouldn't invite too many people to the party!   **BETTER**
You _____ too many people to the party!

6 I must finish this essay tonight!   **GOT**
I _____ this essay tonight!

make, let, help

5 **Put the words in the correct order to make sentences.**

1 learn / by heart / us / the poem / The teacher / made

The teacher made us learn the poem by heart.

2 exams / Talking / nervous / about / me / makes

3 let / get / Mum / me / won't / a part-time job

4 TV / Watching / relax / me / to / helps

5 Our coach / us / train / for two hours / made

6 my bad behaviour / I / apologise / made / to / for / was

6 **Choose the correct answer, A, B or C.**

1 Do you think they will ＿＿ come to the party?
   A let you to
   B let you (circled)
   C made you

2 Joining a sports club can ＿＿ make friends.
   A help to you
   B let you
   C help you to

3 We ＿＿ clear up all the mess ourselves.
   A allowed to
   B were let
   C were made to

4 You ＿＿ go on the trip if I don't want to!
   A can't make me
   B won't be made
   C don't help

5 We ＿＿ look on the internet for ideas.
   A let us
   B were let
   C were allowed to

6 Taking up climbing really ＿＿ more confident.
   A was made   **B** made me   **C** let me

7 In the past, children ＿＿ work from the age of twelve.
   A made them
   B were let
   C were made to

8 My parents said I was too young, so they ＿＿ to the music festival.
   A not allowed to go
   B didn't let me go
   C helped me

7 **Complete the text with the correct form of *help*, *let*, *make* or *be allowed*.**

Drama is a great way to meet new people and improve your self-confidence. Teenager Natalie Jones says, 'I grew up with quite anxious parents. They didn't 1) ＿＿*let*＿＿ me go out very much because they were always worried about me. This 2) ＿＿＿＿ me very shy and lacking in self-confidence.' Natalie saw an advert for a local drama group and decided she would like to join. 'I didn't know if my parents 3) ＿＿＿＿ me do it, but as it was quite close to our home, they said it was fine,' she says. Natalie now says that doing drama has really 4) ＿＿＿＿ her to become more confident. 'When you join a drama group, you 5) ＿＿＿＿ to do all kinds of crazy things,' she says. 'It's hard at first, but after a while it 6) ＿＿＿＿ you much more confident.' Natalie says that her joining the drama group has also 7) ＿＿＿＿ her parents to become less anxious about her. 'They can see that I'm OK, so they worry a lot less,' she says. 'They've even said I will 8) ＿＿＿＿ to go on the drama trip to Paris next year. I can't wait!'

8 **Rewrite the sentences using the word given. Use between two and five words, including the word given.**

1 Dan has to tidy his bedroom every week.   **MAKE**
   Dan's parents ＿＿*make him tidy*＿＿ his bedroom every week.

2 I won't be allowed to stay out that late.   **LET**
   My parents ＿＿＿＿ out that late.

3 Do your teachers let you use the internet in class?   **ALLOWED**
   Are ＿＿＿＿ the internet in class?

4 The prisoners had to work for eight hours a day.   **MADE**
   The prisoners ＿＿＿＿ for eight hours a day.

5 Casper gave me some help with sorting out my computer.   **HELPED**
   Casper ＿＿＿＿ out my computer.

6 I get angry when I see people being cruel to animals.   **MAKES**
   Seeing people being cruel to animals ＿＿＿＿ .

Revision Unit 7

1 Complete the sentences with these words.

camp   coach   ~~competitors~~   direction   feet
mates   opponent   part   trick   way

1 I chatted with the other _competitors_ at the start of the race.
2 I'd love to take _____ in a big sporting event.
3 If you don't like what you are doing, you can change _____ and try something else.
4 We found a good place to set up _____ for the night.
5 It's considered good manners to shake hands with your _____ at the end of the game.
6 My tennis _____ is always telling me that I should be more aggressive when I play.
7 It was hard to find our _____ without a map.
8 I'd like to get a job so that I can stand on my own two _____ .
9 I usually get together with my _____ at the weekend.
10 I don't know why my football team always loses. Maybe getting one or two new players would do the _____ and we might start to win!

2 Complete the definitions with one adjective in each space.

Someone who …
1 enjoys adventures is a_dventurous_ .
2 shows a lot of aggression is a_____ .
3 makes decisions easily is d_____ .
4 has a good imagination is i_____ .
5 enjoys competing and winning is c_____ .
6 tries to protect other people is p_____ .
7 suffers from anxiety is a_____ .
8 is good at supporting other people is s_____ .
9 has a lot of ambition is a_____ .
10 is good at making or creating things is c_____ .

3 Read the article and choose the correct answer, A, B, C or D.

I was always very bad 1) _____ team sports like football and rugby. It really used to 2) _____ me down at school, and I was always 3) _____ of making a fool of myself in front of my peer group. But about six months ago I decided to take up running. I wasn't very 4) _____ on it at first because I found it quite tiring, but as I got fitter, it kind of drew me 5) _____ more and more. I started to find it easier and so I became more 6) _____ about it. Now I would say that I'm 7) _____ to running! I run four or five times a week and I'm very 8) _____ of myself because I've just entered my first marathon. Wish me luck!

1 **A** at   **B** in
   C about   **D** on
2 **A** let   **B** make
   C get   **D** take
3 **A** embarrassed **B** worried
   C anxious   **D** afraid
4 **A** keen   **B** brilliant
   C popular   **D** passionate
5 **A** out   **B** in
   C at   **D** away
6 **A** good   **B** hooked
   C enthusiastic **D** popular
7 **A** hooked   **B** addicted
   C passionate **D** happy
8 **A** proud   **B** happy
   C brilliant   **D** enthusiastic

4 Complete the sentences with the correct form of the words in capitals.

1 I'd love to go to _different_ countries all over the world.　　　　**DIFFER**

2 If you have a .... health problem, you should go to the doctor.　　**PERSIST**

3 The big slide is a very popular .... at the water park.　　**ATTRACT**

4 I wouldn't really like to be ....　　**FAME**

5 I hate being .... on my parents for money!　　**DEPEND**

6 We must do what we can to prevent the .... of the rainforest.　　**DESTROY**

7 My dad was .... when I accidentally broke a window.　　**FURY**

8 It's important to eat healthily and be ....　　**ACT**

9 I have a .... that Clive knows more than he's telling us!　　**SUSPECT**

10 My sister is very .... about trying new things.　　**CAUTION**

5 Choose the correct answer, A, B or C.

1 I wasn't hungry after such a big lunch, so I ...... eat anything in the evening.
A can't　(B) couldn't　C shouldn't

2 My dad can't give us a lift to the station on Saturday, so we ...... get the bus.
A will have to　B had to　C have to

3 Luckily, we ...... score a goal in the last minute, so we won the game.
A ought to　B can　C were able to

4 I need to lose weight, so I ...... stop eating chocolate!
A had to　B must　C better

5 ...... you open the door for me, please?
A Would　B Should　C Must

6 We ...... work hard to prepare for our exams.
A were let　B were made to　C allowed to

7 That kind of stupid behaviour really ...... angry!
A helps me to be　B lets me be
C makes me

8 It was the last day of school, so we ...... go home early.
A were allowed to　B allowed us　C let us

6 Rewrite the sentences using the word given. Use between two and five words, including the word given.

1 I could read when I was four years old.　**ABLE**
I _was able to read_ when I was four years old.

2 We have to train three times a week.　**MAKES**
Our coach .... three times a week.

3 My parents don't let me stay at my friend's house.　**ALLOWED**
I .... at my friend's house.

4 We should start training for the race.　**BETTER**
We .... for the race.

5 It would be a good idea to check the details online.　**OUGHT**
We .... the details online.

6 I wasn't allowed to go out last night.　**LET**
My parents .... out last night.

7 It won't be necessary for you to be there.　**NEED**
You .... there.

8 The teachers didn't let the children play outside.　**MADE**
The children .... inside.

7 Rewrite the sentences correctly.

1 I was made see that my behaviour wasn't acceptable.
I was made to see that my behaviour wasn't
acceptable.

2 When I was younger, I wasn't let to have a TV in my room.
....

3 We've got plenty of time. We don't need hurry.
....

4 Do you think you will able to help us tomorrow?
....

5 I must to spend more time on maths this term!
....

6 We don't allowed to have games consoles at school now.
....

7 Our teachers always make us to turn off our phones in class.
....

8 The concert last night was free, so we don't have to pay.
....

08 Magic numbers

VOCABULARY

1 Complete the sentences with one word in each space.

1 Twenty ___divided___ by two is ten.
2 Six _____ by two is twelve.
3 Seven _____ four is three.
4 Eight _____ two is ten.
5 If you _____ seven to ten, the answer is seventeen.
6 If you _____ five from twenty, the answer is fifteen.

2 Complete the puzzle with words related to maths.

[crossword grid with clue numbers 1, 2, 3, 4, 5, 6. Down 2 spells vertically B A S E]

Across

3 sums that you do with numbers, to work out an answer
5 a way in which a particular feature repeats itself in a regular way
6 the number 0

Down

1 someone who studies maths
2 the number that is used to build a number system, for example ten in the decimal system
4 a set of numbers which increases or decreases in a particular way

3 Look at the pictures and write the words.

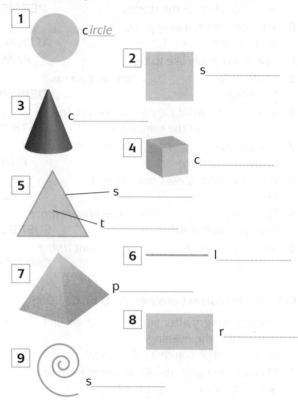

1 c _ircle_
2 s _____
3 c _____
4 c _____
5 s _____
   t _____
6 l _____
7 p _____
8 r _____
9 s _____

4 Complete the sentences with these words.

deep   depth   height   high   length   ~~long~~
wide   width

1 How ___long___ is your garden, from the house right to the bottom of the garden?
2 Giant sequoia trees are the tallest trees in the world. They can reach a _____ of eighty-five metres.
3 Be careful – the water is very _____ here.
4 We measured the _____ of the room, from one side to the other.
5 What's the _____ of the race track, from the start to the finish?
6 At over 800 metres _____, the Burj Khalifa building in Dubai is the tallest building in the world.
7 It's a long way to the other side, so the river is too _____ for me to swim across.
8 You should never dive into a swimming pool until you have checked the _____ of the water.

5 Complete the sentences with these words.

advice equipment experience
imagination ~~information~~ intelligence
knowledge logic news research

1 The book has a lot of _information_ about how the human body works.
2 Scientists are doing a lot of _____ into this disease in the hope that they can find a cure.
3 I always watch the _____ on TV because I like to know what's happening in the world.
4 I've worked in a shop before, but I don't have any _____ of working in a restaurant.
5 Reading books helps to improve your _____ of a particular subject.
6 Can you give me some _____ about which computer I should buy?
7 His argument wasn't clear and there seemed very little _____ to it.
8 Carl draws some amazing pictures – he's got a great _____ .
9 Humans often assume that they have more _____ than other animals, but this isn't true – a lot of animals are very clever, too!
10 You don't need much _____ to do this experiment – just a bowl and a small gas burner.

6 Write C (Countable) or U (Uncountable).

1 We need more **light** in the room!   _U_
2 Please could you make a bit less **noise**?   _____
3 I've been to the USA several **times**.   _____
4 There were over thirty people in the **room**.   _____
5 I wanted to take some notes, but I didn't have any **paper**.   _____
6 I'm sorry, there's no **work** for you here.   _____

7 Choose the correct answers.

1 There are some beautiful *work/*works* of art in the museum.
2 I didn't have enough *time/times* to finish my essay.
3 There were some strange *noise/noises* coming from outside.
4 Remember to turn all the *light/lights* off when you go out.
5 There wasn't much *room/rooms* for people to sit down.
6 The teacher collected in all the exam *paper/papers*.

8 Read the article and choose the correct answer, A, B, C or D.

Take another look at maths

Our modern world relies on mathematics, but very few mathematicians are well-known and maths very rarely makes it into the 1) _____ . Most people think of maths as a scientific subject that uses only 2) _____ and no creativity. However, great mathematical discoveries are a result of 3) _____ as well as science. The Greek Pythagoras was one of the earliest mathematicians. He wanted to gain more 4) _____ of shapes and, using only very simple 5) _____ , he developed some important theorems to calculate the length and area of triangles. These principles are still used in engineering projects all over the world.

Carl Friedrich Gauss was a German mathematician of the eighteenth century whose great 6) _____ was recognised at a young age. He did a lot of 7) _____ into prime numbers. This might not seem very important to us, but in fact the science of prime numbers is used to keep the internet safe from hackers.

Alan Turing was a British mathematician of the twentieth century. During the Second World War he helped to understand German secret codes. This gave the British access to secret 8) _____ about German plans and helped them win the war. After the war, Turing used his 9) _____ of numbers and codes to develop a computing machine – one of the earliest computers. So, maybe we should celebrate great mathematicians more and if you're looking for a career that could make a difference to the world, take my 10) _____ and consider studying maths!

1 A research   B information
  C news   D work
2 A logic   B think
  C brain   D advice
3 A creative   B imagination
  C artistic   D equipment
4 A knowledge   B fact
  C detail   D inform
5 A tool   B machine
  C device   D equipment
6 A intelligent   B intelligence
  C clever   D think
7 A knowledge   B research
  C experiment   D thought
8 A fact   B idea
  C information   D know
9 A experience   B advice
  C knowing   D secret
10 A advise   B support
   C suggest   D advice

GRAMMAR
The passive

1 **Put the words in the correct order to make sentences.**

1 Most / maths / are / children / at / school / taught
   Most children are taught maths at school.

2 The internet / used / for / been / twenty-five / has / years
   _____

3 Calculators / cannot / the exam / used / be / in
   _____

4 All / copied / Tom's answers / were / from / his classmate
   _____

5 chosen / teacher / This textbook / our / was / by
   _____

6 The results / uploaded / the website / to / be / will
   _____

2 **Read the article and choose the correct answer, A, B or C.**

Amazing maths facts

1 Einstein once _____ that pure mathematics is the poetry of logical ideas.
2 An ancient animal bone _____ with marks on it which suggest that people were using mathematics in 35,000 BC.
3 We _____ very much about how maths was used in ancient Egypt.
4 A decimal system of mathematics _____ in China as early as the first century AD.
5 Because of the importance of computers, more mathematicians _____ in the future.
6 Some languages _____ a word for zero.
7 Most early counting systems _____ on the number ten because people have ten fingers which they used for counting.
8 Most of the mathematical notation that _____ today was invented in the sixteenth century.

1	**A** said	**B** was said	**C** has been said
2	**A** found	**B** has found	**C** has been found
3	**A** don't know	**B** aren't know	**C** aren't know
4	**A** is used	**B** was used	**C** was using
5	**A** will needed	**B** will need	**C** will be needed
6	**A** don't have	**B** didn't had	**C** aren't had
7	**A** based	**B** were based	**C** being based
8	**A** used	**B** is used	**C** use

(1 **A** said is circled)

3 **Rewrite the sentences in the passive.**

1 Will they build a new school here?
   Will *a new school be built here* ?

2 I've arranged a visit to a museum for next week.
   A visit _____ .

3 Someone wrote a new book on this subject.
   A new book _____ .

4 Galileo didn't discover this theory.
   This theory _____ .

5 You can find more maths books in the library.
   More maths books _____ .

6 Someone had already solved this problem.
   This problem _____ .

7 They might discover new planets in the future.
   New planets _____ .

8 A celebrity opened the new exhibition.
   The new exhibition _____ .

4 **Complete the text with the correct form of these verbs.**

> become   ~~can / find~~   can / use   have   move
> replace   teach   tell   use

The suanpan, or abacus, is a traditional Chinese counting machine. The first description of a suanpan 1) *can be found* in a text dating back to the second century and the devices 2) _____ in China and other countries since that time.
To use a suanpan, the beads 3) _____ to different positions to indicate different numbers. The beads on the lower part of the machine 4) _____ a value of one and the value for the beads on the upper part is five.
As well as simple adding and subtracting, the suanpan 5) _____ for more complicated tasks such as multiplying and dividing.
Children in China 6) _____ how to use these machines until the 1990s. When electronic calculators first 7) _____ available, they were not very reliable and stories 8) _____ of suanpan operators beating electronic calculators in competitions. Nowadays, however, electronic calculators are much better and faster, so people no longer use suanpans. They 9) _____ by these more modern devices.

Quantifiers and pronouns

5 Complete the sentences with *few*, *a few*, *little* or *a little*.

1 I need _a little_ more time to finish this job.
2 We decided to invite _____ friends round.
3 This theory was popular ten years ago, but there is _____ evidence that it is true.
4 Very _____ people do calculations in their heads nowadays.
5 The disaster happened ten days ago and there is now _____ hope of finding anyone alive.
6 The town is quite small, but there are _____ interesting places to visit there.
7 There's some cheese and _____ bread, so we can make a sandwich.
8 George doesn't go out much and he has very _____ friends.

6 Choose the correct answer, A, B or C.

1 _____ the computers in the library are broken.
  A Either   B Neither   **C** Both of
2 _____ student is given a password to gain access to the school website.
  A All   B Every   C All of
3 There were two questions to choose from in the exam, but I couldn't answer _____ .
  A neither one   B every one   C either one
4 I tried all the machines, but _____ worked.
  A none of them
  B all them
  C either of them
5 _____ students love the new teacher.
  A All of   B All the   C Every
6 I tried calling Sam and Will, but _____ them answered their phone.
  A neither of   B neither   C either of
7 The examiner asked _____ a question in turn.
  A each of us   B each us   C every of us
8 Neither Paul _____ Simon is interested in maths.
  A neither   B or   C nor
9 This torch doesn't work, but it's OK because I've got _____ .
  A other one   B another one   C other
10 Put those books beside _____ on the bookcase.
  A the other ones
  B other ones
  C the another ones

7 Complete the sentences with indefinite pronouns.

1 I haven't had _anything_ to eat all morning, so I'm really hungry!
2 I knocked on the door, but _____ answered.
3 I looked _____ for my calculator, but I couldn't find it.
4 Is there _____ interesting on TV tonight?
5 I looked through the pile of letters, but there was _____ for me.
6 It was a wonderful holiday – _____ was perfect – the beach, the hotel, the weather!
7 We couldn't agree on where to go, so in the end we didn't go _____ .
8 There's _____ under the sofa. What do you think it could be?

8 Complete the text with one word in each space.

View previous comments   Cancel   Share   Post

When it comes to thinking skills, one of the best known brains in the world is the fictional detective Sherlock Holmes. I've read a 1) _few_ of the books and I've seen 2) _____ the films, which I loved. In fact, there's 3) _____ film coming out soon and I'll definitely go and see that, too. Holmes takes on all kinds of criminal cases and 4) _____ of them is different. Sometimes there are plenty of clues to help him, but in other cases there are very 5) _____ clues, so he has to use his intelligence to find the criminal, with a 6) _____ help from his companion, Dr Watson. 7) _____ Holmes nor Watson are police officers, but they always seem to get better results than the police. In fact, there is 8) _____ in the police force who seems as good at solving crimes as Holmes. I'd definitely recommend the Sherlock films. 9) _____ seems to enjoy watching them and I've never met 10) _____ who doesn't like them.

Write a comment   Support

Revision Unit 8

1 Complete the words related to geometry then match them with the pictures a–i.

1 c _i_ r _c_ l _e_ _c_
2 c___ b___ _____
3 c___ n___ _____
4 s_____ r_____ _____
5 r_____ t_____ g l___ _____
6 s p___ r___ l _____
7 t r_____ g l___ _____
8 l___ n___ _____
9 p___ r_____ d _____

a _____
b
c
d
e
f
g
h
i

2 Complete the sentences with one word in each space.

1 That tall building is over 200 metres h _igh_ .
2 If you a_____ twenty to fifty, you get seventy.
3 Are you good at doing mathematical c_____ in your head?
4 The word for the number 0 is z_____ .
5 Are all three s_____ of the triangle the same length?
6 The water in the swimming pool is two metres d_____ .
7 Someone who studies mathematics is a m_____ .
8 If you s_____ fifteen from forty, you get twenty-five.
9 The w_____ of the river is so great here that you can't even see the other side.
10 These snakes can grow to a l_____ of nearly three metres.

3 Complete the sentences with these words.

light   lights   noise   noises   paper   papers
time   times

1 The teacher collected in the ____papers____ at the end of the test.
2 There isn't enough _____ for me to see clearly.
3 I can't concentrate in here – there's too much _____ .
4 Where have you been? I called you five _____ this morning, but you didn't answer your phone.
5 I don't want to sleep in that house again – I heard strange _____ in the night!
6 There was a power cut and all the _____ went out.
7 I've got a pen, but I haven't got any _____ .
8 Hurry up! We don't have much _____ .

4 Choose the correct answer, A, B, C or D.

1 Mathematicians often try to find _____ in numbers.
   A zero   B patterns
   C bases   D calculations
2 We need a lot of expensive _____ to do this job.
   A logic   B research
   C equipment   D imagination
3 I found out some useful _____ about the company.
   A information   B knowledge
   C imagination   D advice
4 What's the _____ of the tallest tree in the world?
   A wide   B high   C height   D long
5 My uncle doesn't have a job at the moment, so he's looking for _____ .
   A work   B works   C task   D job
6 Tom has got a lot of _____ of working with animals.
   A equipment   B experience
   C information   D imagination
7 We need to do some _____ to find out more about the problem.
   A knowledge   B experience
   C advice   D research
8 We use _____ ten in our mathematical system.
   A series   B plus   C pattern   D base

5 Complete the sentences with the correct form of the verbs in brackets.

1 The James Bond books _____were written_____ (write) by Ian Fleming.

2 I couldn't believe it when I _____ (tell) that my uncle was a spy!

3 Last year they _____ (spend) many months trying to find out the secret information.

4 Some very clever gadgets _____ (can / use) to listen to people's conversations.

5 I bought this book last week, but I _____ (not / read) it yet.

6 They have been in the meeting for three hours, but a decision _____ (not / reach) yet.

7 We all hope that a cure for this disease _____ (will / find) soon.

8 By the time I arrived home, all the cake _____ (eat)!

9 You _____ (can / earn) quite a lot of money working as a secret agent.

10 Spies _____ (employ) by governments all over the world nowadays.

6 Rewrite the sentences using the word given. Use between two and five words, including the word given.

1 People eat fish all over the world.   **EATEN**
Fish _____is eaten_____ all over the world.

2 Someone has published a new book on this subject.   **BEEN**
A _____ on this subject.

3 Rembrandt painted this portrait.   **BY**
This _____ Rembrandt.

4 We will announce the results later today.   **BE**
The _____ later today.

5 They clean the windows once a month.   **ARE**
The _____ once a month.

6 You can buy tickets online.   **BOUGHT**
Tickets _____ online.

7 They were upset because a fire had destroyed their home.   **BEEN**
They were upset because their _____ a fire.

8 They arrested the two spies last week.   **WERE**
The _____ last week.

7 Complete the sentences with these words. There are three words which you don't need.

> a few   a little   another   anything   anywhere   both   either   little   neither   none   nor   nothing   other

1 My sister's English is very good, but she still makes _____a few_____ mistakes.

2 I haven't got _____ to wear to the party on Saturday!

3 _____ James nor Dan went to the match last weekend.

4 I'm really hungry, but there's _____ to eat in the fridge!

5 Sara and Emma _____ love the James Bond movies.

6 I can't find my keys _____ !

7 One of my shoes is here, but I don't know where the _____ one is!

8 I've read two books by Ian Fleming, but I didn't like _____ of them.

9 Would you like _____ milk in your coffee?

10 I tried all the batteries, but _____ of them worked!

8 Complete the text with one word in each space.

The World Sudoku Championship 1) _____is_____ organised each year 2) _____ the World Puzzle Federation. The first competition 3) _____ held in 2006 and there has been one 4) _____ year since then. The event started with only a 5) _____ countries represented, but now teams from all over the world take part. The next championship will 6) _____ held in the UK and it is expected to be the biggest yet.

The competition consists of around fifty puzzles which 7) _____ solved 8) _____ the competitors, working to finish as quickly as possible. 9) _____ of the puzzles are easy, of course, but some are more difficult than others.

The most successful players are Thomas Snyder of the USA and Jan Mrozowski from Poland.
The championship has 10) _____ won by 11) _____ of these players three times.

09 ALL change

VOCABULARY

1 Complete the words for different kinds of homes with the missing vowels.

1 v _i_ ll _a_
2 l _ _ ght h _ _ _ _ s _
3 b _ _ ng _ l _ w
4 l _ g c _ b _ n
5 bl _ _ ck _ f fl _ _ ts
6 c _ r _ v _ n
7 _ g l _
8 t _ _ nt
9 t _ rr _ c _ d h _ _ _ s _
10 c _ tt _ g _
11 s _ m _ - d _ t _ ch _ d h _ _ s _
12 h _ _ s _ b _ _ t
13 d _ t _ ch _ d h _ _ s _
14 m _ _ n s _ _ n

2 Complete the definitions with one word in each space.

1 A _cottage_ is a small house in the countryside.
2 A _____ of _____ is a large building where a lot of people live.
3 A _____ is a small house made of wood.
4 A _____ is a very large house.
5 An _____ is a house made of snow and ice.
6 A _____ is a house on one level, with no upstairs.
7 A _____ is a home made of cloth, that you can carry around with you.
8 A _____ house is a house that is joined to other houses on both sides.
9 A _____ is a home on wheels which you can move from place to place.
10 A _____ house is a house that is not joined to any other houses.
11 A _____ is a home on a boat.
12 A _____ is a building on the coast, with a light to warn ships about dangerous rocks.
13 A _____ is a house where you can stay on holiday.
14 A _____ - _____ house is a house that is joined to one other house.

3 Complete the sentences with these words.

curtains cushions dishwasher lampshade
light switch mattress ~~washbasin~~
washing machine

1 Where's the _washbasin_ ? I need to wash my hands.
2 Can you turn the light on, please? The _____ is just by the door.
3 Those colourful _____ look delightful on the sofa!
4 I'll put the dirty clothes in the _____ .
5 That old lamp looks nice with its new _____ .
6 We're having some new _____ made for the window in our bedroom.
7 Can you load the plates and bowls into the _____ , please?
8 This bed is really uncomfortable – I think it needs a new _____ .

4 Choose the correct answers.

1 There's loads of space in this room – it's *tiny/enormous*!
2 Their flat is very small and *spacious/cramped*.
3 Your room is so *messy/tidy*! Why don't you ever put your clothes away?
4 The bathroom is *tiny/roomy* – you can hardly move in it!
5 I like to keep my room nice and *untidy/neat*, so I never leave my clothes on the floor.
6 Although it's only small, their flat feels quite *tiny/roomy*.

5 Complete the texts with one word in each space.

We arrived at the airport early, which was a good thing because we went to the wrong 1) t*erminal* first! Luckily, it wasn't too far to get to the right place. Then our plane was delayed, so we spent over three hours waiting in the 2) d_____ lounge! We were so relieved when they finally announced that our 3) f_____ was leaving. We had bad weather while we were in the air, but luckily we had a very experienced 4) p_____ flying the plane, so it was fine.

I was waiting for my train on the 5) p_____ and when it came into the station I couldn't believe how crowded it was! I managed to find a 6) c_____ with a few seats, but when the 7) g_____ came round to check our tickets, I realised that mine had dropped out of my pocket! Then the train was delayed because a tree had fallen onto the 8) t_____ . The only good thing was that they offered a free meal to all the 9) p_____ in the 10) d_____ c_____ !

I loved every minute of going on a cruise ship, from the minute we sailed out of the 11) p_____ to when we sailed back in three weeks later! The 12) c_____ we slept in was quite spacious and during the day it was lovely sitting up on the 13) d_____ enjoying the sunshine and looking out over the sea. The 14) c_____ were all really nice and friendly, too.

6 Choose the correct answers.

1 I came *to/into/for* contact with loads of people when I was travelling.

2 We had to keep *costs/prices/spend* to a minimum while we were away.

3 You should definitely *take/have/get* advantage of the opportunity to travel.

4 Paris is well-known *to/in/for* its restaurants.

5 We were *going/heading/travelling* for London when the car broke down.

6 It didn't take us long to *go through/get away/go in* customs.

7 We could really relax once we were *on the board/in board/on board* the ship.

8 We should arrive *to/at/for* our destination in about half an hour.

9 We saw some really lovely countryside *on way/at the way/on the way* to Scotland.

10 The city is *named for/called for/named after* an ancient king.

7 Read the blog and choose the correct answer, A, B, C or D.

View previous comments   Cancel   Share   Post

Day 18 – India

We've arrived in India! It's been a tiring day. Our 1) ____ was delayed, unfortunately, and it took us ages to go through 2) ____ when we landed. Then we got on a train and there were no seats in any of the 3) ____ , so we had to stand! Still, the great thing about travelling in this way is that you come into 4) ____ with all kinds of people. Everyone was very friendly, including the 5) ____ who checked our tickets. He didn't charge us more even though we had the wrong tickets! We also saw some amazing sights on the 6) ____ , including wild elephants!

Anyway, we've finally arrived 7) ____ our destination, Jaipur, and we'll soon be 8) ____ for our hostel. We chose quite a cheap one, to keep costs to a 9) ____ , so let's hope it's OK. We'll let you know!

Write a comment   Support

1 A fly   B air
   C travel   D flight

2 A departure   B port
   C customs   D passport

3 A compartments B cabins
   C decks   D platforms

4 A meeting   B contact
   C opportunity   D discussion

5 A pilot   B crew
   C guard   D passenger

6 A way   B path
   C travel   D board

7 A in   B on
   C for   D at

8 A going   B getting
   C heading   D coming

9 A minimum   B maximum
   C small   D reduced

GRAMMAR
Zero, first and second conditionals

1 **Match 1–8 with a–h to make sentences.**

1 If we lived in a bigger flat, _____ *d*
2 If you need money, _____
3 If you could live anywhere in the world, _____
4 We would pay less for electricity _____
5 I get bored _____
6 If I were you, _____
7 We won't move to a bigger house _____
8 We'll go for a walk _____

a when all my friends are away.
b I'd buy a rug to brighten the room up.
c where would you choose?
d we would invite people to stay more often.
e if the weather's fine.
f if we had solar panels on the roof.
g you can get a job.
h unless we win the lottery.

2 **Choose the correct answers.**

1 If you want the room to look more modern, you *have to/had to/will have to* change the furniture.
2 If my dad earned more money, we *lived/will live/would live* in a bigger house.
3 This room feels very small when it *will get/got/gets* messy.
4 If I were you, I *put/'ll put/'d put* some shelves on the wall.
5 We wouldn't live in Madrid if my dad *doesn't/didn't/wouldn't* have a job there.
6 My mum won't let me go out unless I *tidy/will tidy/tidied* my room.
7 I'd have a big TV in my room if I *was/am/will be* allowed.
8 If my dad *gets/will get/got* a job in London, we'll have to move house.
9 If you *can/could/would* speak Chinese, would you like to live in China?
10 If you *won't like/don't like/wouldn't like* these curtains, we'll change them.

3 **Complete the sentences with the correct form of these verbs.**

> apologise be get not let need
> not spend see

1 If my brother _____*gets*_____ a job in New York, he'll move there.
2 We'll buy a cupboard if you _____ somewhere to keep all your things.
3 If you _____ a piece of furniture you really liked, would you buy it?
4 If I don't finish my homework, my mum _____ me go out later.
5 If I were you, I _____ too much money on clothes.
6 I won't invite Jack to my party unless he _____ to me for what he said.
7 Our flat is lovely and light when the weather _____ sunny.

4 **Complete the conversation with the correct form of the verbs in brackets.**

Freya Oh, this is lovely. If I 1) _____*had*_____ loads of money, I 2) _____ (spend) all my time on holiday!

Gina You 3) _____ (get) bored if you 4) _____ (do) nothing all day, every day! You wouldn't enjoy it.

Freya That's not true. If I 5) _____ (can) choose, I 6) _____ (live) in a little cottage by the sea and spend all my time just relaxing.

Gina Wouldn't you miss your friends if you 7) _____ (do) that?

Freya Maybe. But I wouldn't miss school. I hate it when we 8) _____ (have) loads of homework!

Gina Yes, but you 9) _____ (never / get) what you want from life unless you 10) _____ (put) the time and effort in now. If I were you, I 11) _____ (work) hard at school and try to get a good job. If you 12) _____ (manage) to do that, you 13) _____ (be able to) have plenty of holidays!

Freya I guess you're right. But I can still dream!

Third conditional

5 **Match 1–7 with a–g to make sentences.**

1 We wouldn't have missed the train   _d_
2 If we'd bought our tickets in advance, ...
3 We would have sat up on deck   ....
4 If the dining car hadn't been closed, ...
5 We would have caught our flight   ....
6 The trip wouldn't have been so expensive   ....
7 If we'd had more time in New York, ...

a if the weather had been sunny.
b we might have had a meal on the train.
c if we hadn't stayed in five-star hotels.
d if we'd got up earlier.
e we'd have been able to do some shopping.
f if we'd gone to the right terminal.
g they might have been cheaper.

6 **Choose the correct answer, A, B or C.**

1 We would have travelled by plane if it ....
   so expensive.
   A isn't   **(B)** hadn't been   **C** hasn't been

2 If it hadn't rained all the time, we .... our
   holiday more.
   A would enjoy   **B** had enjoyed
   C might have enjoyed

3 If we .... so many souvenirs, we could have gone
   through customs more quickly.
   A don't buy   **B** hadn't bought   **C** didn't buy

4 The guard wouldn't have reported us if .... the
   right tickets.
   A we'd bought   **B** we would have bought
   C we would bought

5 If we'd set out earlier, ... have something to eat at
   the airport.
   A we'd have been able to
   B we were able to
   C we would been able to

6 If the train .... less crowded, we would have
   found a seat.
   A was   **B** would be   **C** had been

7 We could have gone on a longer trip if .... up
   more money.
   A we'd saved up   **B** we would have saved up
   C we would save up

8 I .... so ill on the boat if the sea had
   been calmer.
   A would have felt   **B** wouldn't have felt
   C didn't feel

7 **Complete the text with the correct form of the verbs in brackets.**

Subject: **Missed flight!**

Hi Jenna,
We're still at the airport and it's all my fault. If I
1) _had got up_ (get up) earlier, we
2) .... (leave) home at six this
morning, as we had planned. If we
3) .... (leave) at the right time, we
4) .... (not arrive) with so little time
to spare before our flight. And, of course, if I
5) .... (not be) in such a hurry
to pack this morning, I 6) ....
(remember) that you're not allowed to take liquids
in your hand luggage. Of course, when we went
through the security checks I had to unpack my bag
to take all my shampoo and stuff out! If that
7) .... (not happen), my parents
8) .... (might not be) so stressed.
And, of course, if we 9) .... (all / be)
more relaxed, we probably 10) ....
(not make) the mistake of going to the wrong gate.
So, we've got to wait for six hours for the next
flight – not a good day!

8 **Rewrite the sentences using the word given.
Use between two and five words, including the
word given.**

1 I stayed in because I was tired.   **IF**
   If I hadn't been tired, I wouldn't have stayed in.

2 We didn't have any money so we couldn't
   get a taxi.   **COULD**
   If we'd had some money, ... a taxi.

3 I'm glad we set out early, so the roads
   weren't busy.   **WOULD**
   The roads .... if we'd set out later.

4 I forgot my camera, so I didn't take
   any photos.   **FORGOTTEN**
   If .... my camera,
   I would have taken some photos.

Revision Unit 9

1 Complete the crossword with words related to travel or furniture.

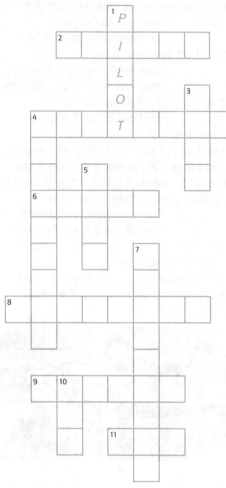

Across

2 a journey in a plane
4 the place where you wait for a train at the station
6 a narrow board attached to a wall that you can put things on
8 a building where people wait to get on a plane
9 a piece of electrical equipment that you can keep food in to keep it cool
11 a piece of equipment for controlling water flow

Down

1 someone who operates the controls of an aircraft
3 all the people who work on a ship or plane
4 someone travelling on a train, boat or plane
5 the top level of a ship that you can walk or sit on
7 a room on a train where you can eat a meal
10 a small carpet that you put on the floor

2 Complete the sentences with these words. There are two words which you don't need.

> carpet   curtains   cushions   dishwasher
> drawer   duvet   light switch   stool   tap
> ~~washbasin~~

1 You can wash your hands in the ___washbasin___ .
2 It's dark in here. Where's the _____ ?
3 I was cold in bed last night. My _____ isn't very thick.
4 Open the _____ so we can see out of the window.
5 The cutlery is in a _____ in the kitchen.
6 I can sit on this little _____ .
7 Remember to load the _____ at the end of the meal.
8 He left muddy footprints on the _____ !

3 Look at the pictures and write the words.

1 ___block of flats___   2 _____

3 _____

4 _____

5 _____   6 _____

4 Choose the correct answers.

1 Their kitchen is lovely and *spacious*/untidy, so there's plenty of room for cooking.

2 They sailed to the USA on a really big ship – it really was *tiny/enormous*!

3 My sister's flat is quite small and *roomy/cramped*.

4 I like my room to be nice and *tidy/tiny*. I can't stand it when it's messy.

5 We should arrive at our *opportunity/destination* at ten thirty.

6 Once everyone is *on/at* board, the ship can leave.

7 The train was delayed due to a problem with the *port/track*.

8 I love coming *into/to* contact with lots of different people.

9 We really need to *have/keep* our costs to a minimum.

10 This is a wonderful opportunity and you should take advantage *of/for* it.

5 Complete the sentences with the correct form of the verbs in brackets.

1 My sister always _____*gets*_____ (get) bad-tempered when she's tired.

2 If I were you, I _____ (save up) and get a new phone.

3 We won't catch our flight unless we _____ (leave) now.

4 I'd become an architect if I _____ (be) better at drawing.

5 We would have arrived by now if we _____ (travel) by plane.

6 Life can be very difficult when you _____ (not have) any money.

7 If I _____ (know) more French, I'd be more confident about speaking to people when I'm on holiday there.

8 If I had known about this museum, I _____ (visit) it when I was in the city last year.

9 If I do well in my exams, I _____ (go) to university.

10 If you had come to the cinema with us yesterday, you _____ (might / enjoy) the film.

6 Rewrite the sentences using the word given. Use between two and five words, including the word given.

1 I'm not very good at singing, so I can't be in a band.   **BETTER**
  If ____*I was better*____ at singing, I could be in a band.

2 My advice is to share a flat with friends.   **YOU**
  If I _____ share a flat with friends.

3 I'm poor, so I don't buy many clothes.   **RICH**
  If I _____ more clothes.

4 We didn't win the money, so we didn't go on holiday.   **MIGHT**
  We _____ if we'd won the money.

5 We won't get to the station on time if we don't leave now.   **UNLESS**
  We won't get to the station on time _____ now.

6 You didn't pack last night, so we left late this morning!   **COULD**
  We _____ this morning if you'd packed last night.

7 It might rain tomorrow, so we'll stay at home.   **IT**
  We'll stay at home _____ tomorrow.

8 I won't call you unless the flight is delayed.   **ONLY**
  I _____ if the flight is delayed.

7 Rewrite the sentences correctly.

1 If I would have bought a ticket, I might have won a prize.
  If I had bought a ticket, I might have won a prize.

2 The party won't be fun unless my friends will come.
  _____

3 If we don't leave soon, we don't get there on time.
  _____

4 I might been able to help you if you'd asked me earlier.
  _____

5 If I were you, I start saving up for your holiday now.
  _____

6 If the train been less crowded, we would have enjoyed the journey more.
  _____

7 I'll text you if the train would be delayed.
  _____

8 If I would have a car, I would be able to drive you to the station.
  _____

VOCABULARY

1 Complete the crossword with words related to science.

Across
```
1 S P E C I E S
```

Across

1 a type of animal or plant
5 someone who does scientific work in order to discover new facts
7 the top or outside layer of something
8 a place where scientists work and do experiments

Down

2 a disease on a part of your body that is caused by a bacteria or virus
3 a scientific instrument that makes small things look bigger
4 to do with medicine
6 a very small structure that all living things are made of

2 Choose the correct answers.

1 Artists often find *inspiration*/infection for their work in nature.
2 Spider silk has some surprising *species/properties*.
3 Wool is not a very strong *structure/material*.
4 You can look at the *structure/power* of a cell under the microscope.
5 Some animals have amazing *powers/inspiration*, like being able to see in the dark.
6 There was something floating on the *structure/surface* of the water.

3 Complete the definitions with these words.

> delicate   durable   flexible   invisible
> man-made   transparent   waterproof

1 Something that is _man-made_ is not natural, but has been produced by people.
2 Something that is _____ can bend easily.
3 If something is _____, you cannot see it.
4 Something that is _____ is not strong and will break easily.
5 If something is _____, it will last for a long time.
6 Something that is _____ does not allow water to pass through it.
7 If something is _____, you can see through it.

4 Read the article and choose the correct answer, A, B, C or D.

We are all accustomed to the 1) _____ of honeybees buzzing around flowers in the summer time. In fact, these amazing creatures have always been an 2) _____ to people for their seemingly endless ability to work. Bees have a very good sense of 3) _____ , so they can find sources of nectar from scented flowers even if they are several kilometres away. Their wings look 4) _____ , but in fact they are very strong – strong enough to carry the weight of the bee and an equal amount of nectar and pollen. Bees can't speak, of course, but they have the 5) _____ to communicate with each other by doing 'dances' to show other members of the hive where flowers can be found. The honey that bees produce has wonderful 6) _____ . It is sweeter than any 7) _____ food and also full of goodness. In the past, it was used for 8) _____ purposes.

1 **A** sight   **B** vision
   C see   **D** view
2 **A** infection **B** inspiration
   C instruction **D** intention
3 **A** smell   **B** hearing
   C taste   **D** vision
4 **A** durable   **B** invisible
   C medical   **D** delicate
5 **A** property   **B** power
   C material   **D** taste
6 **A** structures **B** surfaces
   C properties **D** researchers
7 **A** man-made   **B** durable
   C invisible **D** flexible
8 **A** medicine   **B** treat
   C ill   **D** medical

5 Complete the sentences with one word in each space.

1 Can you speak a bit louder? My ___*hearing*___ isn't very good.
2 I could hear the s_____ of bees in the garden.
3 I love the t_____ of chocolate!
4 You should wear glasses if your s_____ isn't very good.
5 Lambs wool is very soft to t_____ .
6 You have to have perfect v_____ in order to become an aircraft pilot.
7 There was a horrible s_____ of rotten fish!

6 Choose the correct answers.

1 Animal behaviour is a very interesting ⟨topic⟩/topical.
2 It isn't logic/logical to start at number five!
3 We need to find a practice/practical solution to this problem.
4 I'd love to study biology/biological at university.
5 I think she is an inspiration/inspirational singer.
6 Most people nowadays don't believe in magic/magical.
7 This badge is magnet/magnetic, so it will stick to the fridge.

7 Complete the sentences with these words.

> basic   dramatic   electric   microscopic
> panic   ~~plastic~~   scientific

1 Things that are made of ___*plastic*___ don't break down in the soil.
2 The water looks clear to us, but in fact there are millions of _____ creatures in it.
3 The _____ problem is that we don't have enough money.
4 Don't _____ if there's a fire, just leave the building as quickly as possible.
5 The film has a very _____ ending.
6 Some _____ experiments have been done to test this theory.
7 The house was without _____ power for a while during the storm.

8 Complete the sentences with the correct form of the words in capitals.

1 Sometimes ___*biological*___ weapons are used in wars. **BIOLOGY**
2 His new car is a bright _____ blue colour. **METAL**
3 Some scientists have experimented with using _____ energy to power machines. **MAGNET**
4 Many TV documentaries are very _____ for young children. **EDUCATION**
5 I think that one day we will all drive _____ cars. **ELECTRICITY**
6 I've never been very _____ – I can't even draw a simple picture! **ART**

9 Complete the article with the correct form of the words in brackets.

Bird song is one of the 1) ___*natural*___ (nature) sounds we associate with summer. It has always been enjoyed and admired for its beauty and has been 2) _____ (inspiration) to poets over the centuries. Different birds produce a great variety of songs – from the sweet and 3) _____ (music) song of the blackbird to the loud and 4) _____ (drama) hoot of the owl. However, there are simple 5) _____ (biology) reasons for why birds sing. 6) _____ (science) studies have shown that birds sing either to attract a mate, to make a claim on their territory or to warn other birds of danger. So there is nothing 7) _____ (magic) about bird song – it is just a form of communication like any other.

GRAMMAR
-ing forms and infinitives

1 Choose the correct answers.

1 I enjoy *to visit/visiting* the zoo.
2 Some insects seem *to move/moving* very quickly.
3 Do you expect some species of animal *to become/ becoming* less common in the future?
4 I think we had better *go/to go* home now.
5 I really don't know what *do/to do* now.
6 Professor Higgins agreed *to help/helping* us.
7 Tim prefers *work/working* alone.
8 I can't imagine *to live/living* in a world without animals.

2 Complete the sentences with the correct form of the verbs in brackets.

1 These creatures appear ___*to have*___ (have) some amazing powers.
2 My uncle wants me _____ (help) him with some experiments.
3 Carl suggested _____ (take) a camera with us so we could take some photos.
4 We've decided _____ (go) to South America next year.
5 How do you know about this? It's supposed _____ (be) a secret!
6 Jack has invited me to his party, but I'd prefer _____ (watch) a DVD with a few friends.
7 I'm not sure how _____ (get) to the city centre by bus.
8 We could watch TV, but I'd rather _____ (play) on the computer.
9 Does the experiment involve _____ (kill) animals?
10 _____ (use) animals in medical experiments is wrong in my opinion.

3 Complete the sentences with the correct form of these words. Add any other words that are necessary.

> better / take   decide / do   forget / water
> hate / be   involve / work   love / watch
> rather / study   supposed / go

1 Scientists wanted to find out more about these creatures, so they ___*decided to do*___ some experiments.
2 I'd love to do a job that _____ with animals.
3 I'm really interested in nature and I _____ documentaries about animals.
4 Come on – hurry up! I _____ late!
5 I think we _____ some food with us because we might get hungry later.
6 Why is your little brother still up? He _____ to bed at seven o'clock!
7 All my plants died because I _____ them.
8 My parents want me to do medicine at university, but I _____ biology.

4 Complete the text with one word in each space.

| Subject: **New job!** |

Hi Jack,
Guess what? I've got a job working at the zoo in the summer holidays! I decided 1) ___*to*___ apply because my brother worked there last year and he said it's really interesting. The only problem is that they want 2) _____ to work in the snake house! I'm not very happy about that. I don't really like snakes and I wouldn't know 3) _____ to do if one escaped! I 4) _____ rather work with the elephants! They 5) _____ supposed to be really intelligent animals, aren't they? Anyway, I guess I 6) _____ better accept any job they're willing to give me. I just hope I don't 7) _____ to touch the snakes!

have/get something done

5 Choose the correct answer, A, B or C.

1 I went to the dentist yesterday and _____ .
   A had cleaned my teeth
   B got my teeth clean
   C had my teeth cleaned

2 If you can't see that, you should _____ .
   A get your eyes tested
   B have your eyes test
   C have your eyes testing

3 My computer's broken, so I'm _____ .
   A getting repaired   B having repair it
   C getting it repaired

4 My sister is really upset. She _____ last Saturday.
   A stole her bag   B had her bag stolen
   C got her bag stolen

5 Have you _____ yet?
   A had decorated your bedroom
   B got your bedroom decorate
   C had your bedroom decorated

6 Your hair is too long. You should _____ .
   A get cut   B have cut it
   C get it cut

7 They _____ by kids playing football.
   A got some windows broken
   B had some windows broken
   C got break some windows

6 Complete the sentences with the correct form of have/get something done.

1 We _get the windows cleaned_ (get / the windows / clean) every week.

2 My glasses are broken, so I need to _____ (have / them / mend).

3 My dad _____ (have / his car / take) from outside his office last week.

4 You can order a new computer online and _____ (get / it / deliver) to your home.

5 When we do an experiment, we always _____ (have / the results / check).

6 That's a lovely photo. Why don't you _____ (get / it / frame)?

7 I had to _____ (have / a tooth / take out) at the dentist yesterday.

8 After the burglary last month, we _____ (have / new locks / fit) on all the doors.

7 Complete the text with the correct form of have and these verbs and phrases.

> a mini science lab / install   a TV / fix
> the walls / paint   your dream / make
> ~~your perfect room / design~~

Fancy a new bedroom? Just sit back and relax. You can 1) _have your perfect room designed_ by our expert designers. Just tell them what you want. For example, you can 2) _____ to the wall opposite your bed, so you can sit in bed and watch your favourite programmes. If you're into science, why not 3) _____ in one corner of the room? You can 4) _____ any colour of your choice. Once you've decided on your dream room, just relax and 5) _____ a reality by our expert fitters.

8 Rewrite the sentences using the word given. Use between two and five words, including the word given.

1 The hairdresser cut my hair yesterday.   **HAD**
   I _____ _had my hair cut_ _____ yesterday.

2 Someone stole my microscope from the laboratory.   **STOLEN**
   I _____ from the laboratory.

3 You should ask someone to check your computer for viruses.   **GET**
   You should _____ for viruses.

4 I'd prefer to study languages.   **RATHER**
   I _____ languages.

5 You should turn the music down a bit.   **BETTER**
   You _____ the music down a bit.

6 We don't know what we can do about this problem.   **TO**
   We don't know _____ about this problem.

1 **Unscramble and write the words related to science.**

1 Cotton is not a very strong __material__ (atremial).

2 Your body is made up of millions of _____ (lelcs).

3 We looked at the skin under a _____ (mcriocspoe).

4 It's better to buy things that are _____ (draubel) because they will last for a long time.

5 We studied the _____ (rsutctrue) of the eye in our biology lesson.

6 The curtains were so thin that they were almost _____ (anstrpaertn).

7 Oil will float on the _____ (ursfcea) of water.

8 You should go to the doctor if you have a _____ (deicmla) problem.

9 Metal is strong, but not very _____ (lefelibx).

10 In stories, people can sometimes make themselves _____ (isvniielb).

2 **Complete the sentences with these words. There are two words which you don't need.**

> hear   hearing   see   ~~sight~~   smell   sound
> taste   touch   vision

1 Seeing thousands of these butterflies in the air is an amazing __sight__ .

2 My grandad always has the TV very loud because he's got such bad _____ .

3 Silk is so lovely and soft to _____ !

4 I could hear the _____ of an aeroplane in the distance.

5 Do you have a _____ of what life will be like in thirty years?

6 The sauce had a delicious creamy _____ .

7 There was a horrible _____ when he took his boots off!

3 **Complete the text with the correct form of the words in brackets.**

mailbox   Today | Mail | Calendar | Contacts

Reply | Reply All | Forward | Delete

To: **Andy**   Subject: **Guess what!**

Hi Andy,
I saw an amazing
1) __sight__ (see)
down by the river this
morning! A kingfisher!
Have you ever seen
one? Their wings
are a really bright
2) _____ (metal) blue colour. This one
was sitting above the river, then it suddenly did
a 3) _____ (drama) dive into the water
and caught a fish! It was really 4) _____
(magic) to watch! I've just found some
information about them online and it seems they
have a 5) _____ (nature) ability to catch
fish, even when they're very young. I think they
are 6) _____ (inspiration) creatures!
Love,
Carly

4 **Choose the correct answer, A, B, C or D.**

1 There were some dirty marks on the _____ of the glass.
  A structure   (B) surface
  C property   D power

2 There are thousands of different _____ of insects.
  A creatures   B animals
  C cells   D species

3 The doctor gave me some cream to treat the _____ on my skin.
  A infection   B illness
  C sickness   D medical

4 Scientific experiments are usually carried out in a _____ .
  A microscope   B laboratory
  C material   D surface

5 One useful _____ of rubber is that it is very flexible.
  A property   B character
  C skill   D ability

6 I'd love to work as a _____ and try to discover new drugs.
  A species   B laboratory
  C researcher   D medical

5 **Choose the correct answer, A, B or C.**

1 Do you enjoy _____ new places?
   A discover   **B** to discover   (**C**) discovering

2 _____ too much chocolate isn't good for you.
   A Eat   **B** Eating   **C** To eat

3 I've decided _____ a doctor.
   A to become   **B** become   **C** becoming

4 I don't know how _____ this machine!
   A use   **B** to use   **C** using

5 My parents expect me _____ with jobs at home.
   A to help   **B** helping   **C** help

6 I haven't got any money, but I would rather _____ a weekend job.
   A not get   **B** don't get   **C** can't get

7 It's late. I think we had better _____ playing music now.
   A to stop   **B** stop   **C** stopping

8 Owls are able _____ their prey in the dark.
   A see   **B** seeing   **C** to see

6 **Complete the messages with one word in each space.**

Messages   **Jane**

Help! There's a huge spider in the shower! I don't know what 1) ___*to*___ do!

Oh, no! I guess you had 2) _____ try and move it!

No way! I don't want 3) _____ touch it! I'd 4) _____ just not have a shower!

Is your sister there? She might know 5) _____ to get it out.

No, she's gone to the police station. She 6) _____ her bag stolen this morning, so she's gone to report it. Guess it's just a bad day all round! :(

7 **Cross out one incorrect word in each sentence.**

1 I enjoy to spending time with my grandparents.

2 The guide showed us where we to go.

3 My friend always wants to chat online, but I would to prefer to meet face-to-face.

4 I lent Mike £5 last week, so he had don't better not ask me for any more money!

5 Jack wants me to go out to the cinema with him, but I would rather to stay at home.

6 My parents want me to I become a scientist.

7 The exam is tomorrow, so you had better and revise this evening!

8 We're cutting up a mouse in our biology lesson tomorrow, but I would don't rather not watch!

8 **Rewrite the sentences using the word given. Use between two and five words, including the word given.**

1 The dentist checked my teeth yesterday.   **GOT**
   I ___*got my teeth checked*___ yesterday.

2 I think you ought to phone Sally.   **BETTER**
   I think _____ Sally.

3 The doorman told us where we should put our coats.   **TO**
   The doorman told us _____ our coats.

4 I don't want to have a big meal.   **RATHER**
   I _____ a big meal.

5 Someone broke Sara's glasses last week.   **BROKEN**
   Sara _____ last week.

6 You should ask someone to check the car as soon as possible.   **GET**
   You should _____ as soon as possible.

7 We mustn't be late!   **HAD**
   We _____ late!

8 Everyone says it's a great film!   **SUPPOSED**
   It _____ a great film!

VOCABULARY

1 Choose the correct answers.

1 My mum told me to stop messing *up/around* and get on with my homework.
2 Is that story true or did you make it *up/out*?
3 The magazine *comes/gets* out every Thursday.
4 Those drawings are really good, so don't throw them *up/away*.
5 If you want a career in the arts, you just have to go *on/for* it!
6 I'd love to *do/have* a go at doing computer animations.
7 How do you *make/rate* our chances of winning?
8 You can *take/make* my place on the workshop if you want.
9 I had plans for a new computer game, but they didn't *go/come* to much.
10 Do you think your dreams will ever *come/get* true?

2 Complete the sentences with one word from each box.

> artistic cartoon fantasy ~~learning~~ vivid

> characters ~~experience~~ imagination skill world

1 When we visited the film studio, they taught us a lot about film-making. It was a great *learning experience*.
2 The film creates a complete _____ of castles and monsters.
3 James is really good at writing stories. He's got a very _____ _____ .
4 It's an animated film with _____ _____, not actors.
5 You must need a lot of _____ _____ to do those very detailed drawings.

3 Choose the correct answer, A, B, C or D.

Animation workshops

Do you love watching 1) _____ on TV? Or maybe you have your favourite 2) _____ that you read every week? If you would like to learn how to turn your hobby into a career, come to one of our animation workshops!

People often make the mistake of thinking that to work in animation you have to be good at 3) _____. It isn't true. Of course, having a lot of artistic 4) _____ is useful, but it isn't absolutely necessary. There are plenty of other ways to create great animated 5) _____ – think of Wallace and Gromit or Toy Story! One thing you do need, though, is lots of ideas and a vivid 6) _____ so that you can 7) _____ some great story lines!

If you've got a passion for animation, sign up for a workshop now! You'll be 8) _____ away! It's a great learning 9) _____ and at the end of the three days you'll have some fantastic 10) _____ to take home with you!

1	A	sketches	B	drawings
	C	cartoons	D	comics
2	A	drawing	B	comic
	C	character	D	paint
3	A	drawing	B	skill
	C	experience	D	sketch
4	A	skill	B	fantasy
	C	artwork	D	drawing
5	A	paints	B	characters
	C	crayons	D	imagination
6	A	imagination	B	experience
	C	skill	D	artwork
7	A	go over	B	make up
	C	do up	D	get on
8	A	taken	B	pushed
	C	blown	D	pulled
9	A	skill	B	imagination
	C	experience	D	world
10	A	crayons	B	imagination
	C	paints	D	artwork

(1 C cartoons — circled)

4 Unscramble and write the words related to entertainment.

1 Do you like _classical_ (lascalsic) music?
2 I'd love to go to a film _____ (ripermeè) and see all the stars!
3 Some very famous _____ (tsac) have performed in this theatre.
4 Wembley Stadium is a very good _____ (neveu) for concerts.
5 My grandma appeared in a _____ (whos) on Broadway when she was young!

5 Complete the email with these words.

audience   box office   interval   ~~open–air~~
row   seat   sold out   stage

mailbox

Today | Mail | Calendar | Contacts

Reply | Reply All | Forward | Delete

To: **Jo**   Subject: **Rock-n-roll!**

I saw a great rock concert last night! It was at an 1) _open-air_ amphitheatre and luckily for us it didn't rain! I had a great 2) _____ right near the front. I wasn't in the front 3) _____ , but I was still quite close to the band. It was so exciting when the lights went out and the band came onto the 4) _____ ! It was an amazing concert and the 5) _____ went wild when the band played some of their big hits. I was talking to some other fans during the 6) _____ and it seems there's another concert coming soon. Do you fancy going? We should be able to get some tickets at the 7) _____ because I don't think it's 8) _____ yet.

6 Choose the correct answers.

1 This arena is a great (setting)/fame for rock concerts.
2 I love that band – I'm a member of their music–lovers/fan club.
3 I'd like to know a little bit more about the comedy/background to this show.
4 The band sounded awful because the audience/acoustics were so bad.
5 A lot of young people dream of achieving fame/stage.
6 A lot of famous musicians/music-lovers have performed in this venue.
7 My cousin goes to loads of concerts – he's a real music-lover/fan club!

7 Read the notice and choose the correct answer, A, B or C.

Drama Club

This notice is for everyone involved in the school 1) ____ . Don't forget that there's a 2) ____ tomorrow evening after school. And it's for everyone – people playing the main 3) ____ and those who have just got small parts. Please make sure you're there on time! You should all know your 4) ____ by now, but someone will be there to help you if you forget one or two words. It's really important to know all your words before you get up on the 5) ____ in front of a live 6) ____ . And don't forget that we're performing a 7) ____ , so come in a good mood and ready to have a laugh!
We're still looking for people to help out with other aspects of the show. We need people to help put out 8) ____ in the hall and we'd also like some volunteers to help serve tea and coffee during the 9) ____ . We're also looking for one or two more 10) ____ for the band, so if you can play the guitar or violin, please come along!

1	**A** role	(**B**) play	**C** stage
2	**A** rehearsal	**B** première	**C** setting
3	**A** lines	**B** acts	**C** roles
4	**A** acts	**B** lines	**C** settings
5	**A** stage	**B** play	**C** show
6	**A** fan club	**B** audience	**C** venue
7	**A** classical	**B** role	**C** comedy
8	**A** seats	**B** shows	**C** lines
9	**A** audience	**B** interval	**C** background
10	**A** musicians	**B** music-lovers	**C** fan clubs

GRAMMAR
Reported speech

1 Choose the correct answers.

1 'I love that comedy show.'
Sara said that she (loved)/loves that comedy show.

2 'There won't be any tickets left.'
Jack told us that there won't/wouldn't be any tickets left.

3 'I've never been to a concert at that venue.'
Paula said she has never been/had never been to a concert at that venue.

4 'The tickets aren't selling very quickly.'
Mark said that the tickets aren't selling/weren't selling very quickly.

5 'You must go and watch him perform.'
Ana said that we must/had to go and watch him perform.

6 'You should listen to their music.'
Pete said that we should/will listen to their music.

7 'I watched a play on TV the previous night.'
Carla said that she has watched/had watched a play on TV the previous night.

8 'You ought to go to more live performances.'
Leo told me that I ought to/had ought to go to more live performances.

2 Rewrite the sentences in reported speech.

1 'You're a great singer.'
Paul told _____me that I was_____ a great singer.

2 'The show has already started.'
They said that the show _____.

3 'It will be difficult to get tickets.'
Sam said that _____ to get tickets.

4 'We must leave at five.'
My dad said that _____ at five.

5 'All the actors gave amazing performances.'
Jess said that all the actors _____ amazing performances.

6 'Let's go for a pizza before the show.'
Liam suggested that we _____ for a pizza before the show.

7 'You ought to practise your guitar more.'
My mum told me that _____ my guitar more.

8 'I'm not going to the concert.'
My brother told me that _____ to the concert.

3 Read the conversation and complete the text with the correct verb forms. Add any other necessary words.

Carl Hi, Ana. How are you?

Ana Fed up! I really wanted to get into the school orchestra this year, but they didn't accept me.

Carl Oh, that's a shame, because you can play the violin really well.

Ana Thanks. But it doesn't matter. I'll probably get in next year. I know I ought to practise a bit more.

Carl Hey, I know something that will cheer you up. There's a concert on at the O2 Arena on Saturday.

Ana Great! Let's go and have a coffee and talk about it!

Ana said that she 1) _____was_____ fed up because 2) _____ to get into the school orchestra, but they 3) _____ . Carl said that it 4) _____ because Ana 5) _____ the violin really well. Anna thanked him and said that it 6) _____ . She said she 7) _____ the following year. She said that she knew that 8) _____ practise more. Carl said he 9) _____ something that 10) _____ Ana up. He told her that 11) _____ a concert on at the O2 Arena that Saturday. Ana suggested that 12) _____ and had a coffee and talked about it.

4 Complete the blog post with one word in each space.

💬 View previous comments   Cancel   Share   Post

Well, I guess it's my lucky day! I went for an audition for the X-Factor today and guess what? I got in! The judges listened to me singing, then told 1) _____me_____ that I had a lot of talent and that I 2) _____ performed really well! One of the judges said that I 3) _____ the best singer they'd heard that day! How about that? I talked to the judges afterwards and told 4) _____ about my dreams of becoming a famous singer. They 5) _____ I've definitely got what it takes, but they told me I 6) _____ to take my singing more seriously if I really wanted to make it big! They suggested that I 7) _____ get a personal singing teacher. They also said 8) _____ I ought to think about my image more. Any ideas, anyone?

Write a comment   Support

Reporting orders and requests

5 Choose the correct answers.

1 'Don't forget to post the letter!'
My mum (reminded)/begged me to post the letter.

2 'Please, please come with us!'
My friends *ordered/begged* me to go with them.

3 'Stand back!'
The police officers *ordered/allowed* us to stand back.

4 'You should work harder.'
My teacher *permitted/advised* me to work harder.

5 'Please can you help me?'
My friend *asked/warned* me to help her.

6 'Yes, of course you can go to the concert.'
My parents *persuaded/allowed* me to go to the concert.

6 Choose the correct answer, A, B or C.

1 The police ordered the crowd ____ .
A that they leave
B (to leave)
C leave

2 Martin ____ for him.
A said me to wait
B asked to wait
C told me to wait

3 My friend ____ anyone her secret.
A told me don't tell
B asked not to tell
C warned me not to tell

4 My parents ____ to the festival.
A didn't allow me to go
B didn't permit me go
C didn't allow I go

5 My teacher ____ all my revision until the last minute.
A encouraged me don't leave
B advised me not to leave
C warned me that I don't leave

7 Rewrite the sentences in reported speech.

1 'You really should study music.'
My teachers persuaded *me to study music* .

2 'Don't be late home.'
My dad warned me ____ .

3 'Can you lend me some money?'
My sister asked me ____ .

4 'Hand your homework in on Monday.'
The teacher told us ____ .

5 'You shouldn't stay up so late.'
Sam advised me ____ .

6 'Stop making so much noise!'
My dad ordered us ____ .

7 'Remember to bring your sports clothes to school.'
The teacher reminded us ____ .

8 'Don't give up playing the guitar.'
My parents persuaded me ____ .

8 Rewrite the sentences using the word given. Use between two and five words, including the word given.

1 Jack told me I should take up acting.
ENCOURAGED
Jack *encouraged me to take up* acting.

2 'Please don't eat all the cake,' Martha said to her friends. **ASKED**
Martha asked ____ all the cake.

3 'Remember to do the shopping,' Paul's aunt said to him. **REMINDED**
Paul's aunt ____ the shopping.

4 'I don't think you should accept the role', Tara's agent said to her. **ADVISED**
Tara's agent ____ the role.

5 'Do Exercise 5 for homework,' the teacher said to the students. **TOLD**
The teacher ____ Exercise 5 for homework.

6 'Don't spend all your money,' my mum said to me. **WARNED**
My mum ____ all my money.

Revision Unit 11

1 Complete the sentences with one word in each space.

1 I'd never performed on a s _tage_ in front of so many people before.

2 We had a great view because we were sitting in the front r_____ .

3 We went to an e_____ of landscape paintings at the art gallery.

4 There's a fifteen minute i_____ in the middle of the performance.

5 The show was a great success and the a_____ all cheered at the end.

6 To be a writer, you need a very vivid i_____ .

2 Complete the definitions with these words. There are two words which you don't need.

> acoustics   box office   fan club   musician
> music-lover   ~~première~~   role   seat

1 A _première_ is the first performance of a play or film.

2 A _____ is someone who plays music.

3 A _____ is a place where you can buy tickets for a performance.

4 A _____ is a chair you sit on to watch a performance.

5 A _____ is an organisation for people who like a particular singer, actor, etc.

6 A _____ is someone who enjoys listening to music.

3 Choose the correct answers.

1 I did a rough (sketch)/paint of the house.

2 Some children like to live in a fantasy place/world.

3 What day does the magazine usually come/go out?

4 Do you dream of achieving stage/fame?

5 I want that old comic – don't throw it away/off!

6 Going on the course was a great learn/learning experience.

7 One day your dreams may get real/come true!

8 If you want to become a famous pop singer, just go at/go for it!

4 Read the advert and choose the correct answer, A, B, C or D.

Brigstock Festival

There's something for everyone at the Brigstock Festival of the Arts. You can hear all kinds of music, from 1) ____ to rock. There's a great variety of 2) ____ in different 3) ____ all around the town, including the magnificent Royal Hall, which has wonderful 4) ____ . There are also 5) ____ performances in Queen's Park, which is a wonderful 6) ____ for concerts.

There's plenty for kids to do, too. There are play areas where they can 7) ____ around with paints or crayons. There are also more formal workshops where they can 8) ____ a go at drawing cartoon 9) ____ and 10) ____ up stories about them. You should book early for these, as they tend to get sold 11) ____ quite quickly.

For more information or to find out more about the 12) ____ to the festival, visit our website at www.brigstockarts.co.uk.

1	A acoustics		(B) classical	
	C audience		D animation	
2	A shows		B lines	
	C roles		D rows	
3	A plays		B rehearsals	
	C venues		D stages	
4	A background		B setting	
	C acoustics		D fame	
5	A air		B open-air	
	C interval		D rehearsal	
6	A setting		B role	
	C play		D show	
7	A touch		B mess	
	C go		D use	
8	A use		B take	
	C make		D have	
9	A lines		B roles	
	C characters		D plays	
10	A getting		B going	
	C having		D making	
11	A out		B up	
	C off		D away	
12	A setting		B background	
	C play		D seat	

5 Rewrite the sentences in reported speech.

1 'I love going to the theatre!'
Mary said that ___*she loved*___ going to the theatre.

2 'I've already seen that film.'
Stacey said that she _____ that film.

3 'We aren't going to the concert.'
They told me they _____ to the concert.

4 'There may be some tickets left.'
They told us at the box office that there
_____ some tickets left.

5 'You must see them perform live!'
Clare told me that I _____ them perform live.

6 'I'll book the tickets online.'
Sam said that he _____ the tickets online.

7 'Let's watch a DVD.'
Paul suggested that we _____ a DVD.

8 'You ought to read this book.'
Sara told me that I _____ this book.

6 Choose the correct answer, A, B or C.

1 'Tidy your room immediately!'
My mum _____ my room immediately.
(A) told me to tidy
B said me to tidy
C asked me tidy

2 'Please, please help us!'
They _____ them.
A persuaded me help
B begged me to help
C ordered me to help

3 'Don't let the microphone get wet.'
Dan _____ the microphone get wet.
A permitted me to let
B advised me don't let
C warned me not to let

4 'Yes, you can go to the festival.'
My parents _____ to the festival.
A allowed me to go
B permitted me go
C reminded me to go

5 'Can you pay for the tickets?'
Rob _____ for the tickets.
A advised me to pay
B persuaded me that I pay
C asked me to pay

6 'Remember, you mustn't be late.'
My dad _____ late.
A persuaded me to be
B reminded me not to be
C encouraged me to be

7 Complete the text with one word in each space.

HOW DO YOU BECOME A SUCCESSFUL COMEDIAN?

We spoke to young comedian Andy Roberts. He told us that he 1) ___*had*___ started performing at a young age. He said a friend had advised him 2) _____ become a comedian because he 3) _____ always making jokes at school. It seems his parents weren't so keen. They advised him 4) _____ to try and make a living from performing, but Andy's heart was set on a career in comedy and he knew it was something he 5) _____ to do. At the age of sixteen, an agent suggested that he 6) _____ start by trying to do some shows in small venues close to home. The agent said 7) _____ Andy would know fairly soon whether he was popular with audiences. Audiences loved him and a lot of people who saw his early shows wrote to him and encouraged 8) _____ to continue performing. He now performs all over the country and has just been offered his own TV show!

8 Rewrite the sentences using the word given. Use between two and five words, including the word given.

1 'I've never heard of that band.'   **HAD**
Emily said that she ___*had never heard*___ of that band.

2 'You should become a professional musician,' my mum said to me.   **ADVISED**
My mum _____ a professional musician.

3 'Let's meet outside the theatre,' Mike said.   **SUGGESTED**
Mike suggested that _____ outside the theatre.

4 'You should go to drama college,' Stella's dad told her.   **ENCOURAGED**
Stella's dad _____ to drama college.

5 Jack thought the show started at seven.   **THINK**
'I _____ at seven', Jack said.

6 'Please don't mess around during rehearsals,' the teacher said to us.   **TO**
The teacher asked _____ during rehearsals.

VOCABULARY

1 Choose the correct answers.

1 Tom will never *argue/admit* when he's wrong about something.
2 What's your *view/speech* on asking for help with your homework? Do you think it's always wrong?
3 Her essay *concluded/discussed* that cheating in exams is never acceptable.
4 I think we should *discuss/argue* this topic further.
5 What's the best way to *conclude/prepare* for exams?
6 Nathan is always *arguing/discussing* with his dad about politics – they never agree!
7 Paul is quite an interesting *discussion/individual*.

2 Complete the sentences with the correct form of the words in capitals.

1 James put forward some very convincing _arguments_ in his speech. **ARGUE**
2 Elena always speaks with great _____ . **CLEAR**
3 Good _____ is really important when you're speaking in public. **PREPARE**
4 You should try to bring all your ideas together in your _____ . **CONCLUDE**
5 We had some very interesting _____ about human rights. **DISCUSS**
6 I'd be terrified if I had to give a _____ in public. **SPEAK**

3 Complete the puzzle and find the mystery word.

	1 E	Q	U	A	L	I	T	Y
2								
3								
4								
5								

1 a situation in which all people have the same rights
2 the quality of being strong
3 a duty you have to do something or be in charge of something
4 a feeling of admiration for someone because of their qualities or skills
5 the quality of being honest

Mystery word: _____

4 Complete the sentences with these words.

> advice   difference   ~~freedom~~   rights   skills
> truth

1 The people protested in the streets and demanded _freedom_ .
2 In some countries, human _____ aren't respected.
3 Do you believe that an individual can really make a _____ in the world?
4 I often ask my parents what I should do, but I don't often follow their _____ !
5 I try to be honest, but sometimes it's kinder not to tell the _____ .
6 I really enjoy learning new _____ .

5 Complete the text with one word in each space.

Eastleigh Youth Club

At Eastleigh Youth Club we believe 1) _in_ helping young people to grow into confident adults. Our members can take 2) _____ in lots of fun activities or just chill out and chat. We run football teams for boys and girls. We believe that team sports help you learn to stick 3) _____ and stand up 4) _____ each other. We don't focus 5) _____ winning, though. We think it's important to take pride 6) _____ doing well, but also accept losing with a smile! At Eastleigh we stand 7) _____ fairness. We encourage our members to show respect 8) _____ each other and to speak 9) _____ if they see others behaving badly. We try to help all our young people to have confidence 10) _____ themselves and to feel confident about the future.

6 Choose the correct answers.

1 It's a very *formal/informal* event, so you can wear jeans if you want.

2 You must make sure your writing is *legible/illegible* in the exam.

3 These creatures are so small that they are *visible/invisible* without a microscope.

4 My brother annoys me because he's so *mature/immature* – he laughs at really stupid things!

5 It isn't *responsible/irresponsible* to throw paper in the bin – you should recycle it!

6 You might win a prize if you're *lucky/unlucky*!

7 I can't understand this decision – it seems *rational/irrational* to me!

8 Going for a pizza together was *planned/unplanned* – we just decided on our way home that we would do it!

7 Complete the sentences with the negative form of the adjectives in brackets.

1 I find learning *irregular* verbs very difficult! (regular)

2 I think it's very _____ to leave without saying goodbye to everyone! (polite)

3 My mum is always complaining that my bedroom is _____ . (tidy)

4 Our old car was very _____ – it was always breaking down! (reliable)

5 You don't get any marks for an _____ answer. (correct)

6 I think it's _____ not to tell a shop assistant when they've made a mistake with your change. (honest)

7 Why are you going to go all the way home when you have to be back here in an hour? It's _____ . (logical)

8 My dad complained to the restaurant because he was _____ with his meal. (satisfied)

8 Complete the sentences with the correct form of these words.

> correct   formal   legal   necessary
> possible   ~~reliable~~   responsible   visible

1 No one will give Tyler a job because he's so ___*unreliable*___ . He never arrives on time!

2 It wasn't really an interview – more of an _____ chat about the job.

3 It's _____ to drive a car without a driving licence.

4 I think it's _____ to have pets if you don't have time to look after them.

5 We've already put up ten posters and I think that's enough. It's _____ to put up any more.

6 There's too much vocabulary here – it's _____ to learn it all!

7 I thought Marco was from Portugal, but that was _____ – he's from Spain.

8 The mountain was _____ because of the thick fog.

9 Complete the blog post with the correct form of the words in brackets.

💬 View previous comments   Cancel   Share   Post

Film downloads – my view

What are your views on downloading music and films without paying? We all know it's 1) ___*illegal*___ , but some people argue that it's OK. They think it isn't 2) _____ (honest) because it isn't really like stealing. They also believe  they can get away with it. Very few people are 3) _____ (luck) enough to be caught, as it's virtually 4) _____ (possible) for the police to keep an eye on what everyone's doing online. I don't agree with this point of view, though. I think it's 5) _____ (fair) to the actors who've worked hard to make films when we just download and watch them without paying. It's also 6) _____ (necessary), as it really isn't very expensive to download films legally. Also, I think that if you're 7) _____ (satisfy) with the amount you have to pay for a movie, you should speak up and complain rather than breaking the law. So, for me, taking anything without paying for it is always 8) _____ (accept). Let me know what you think!

Write a comment   Support

GRAMMAR
Modal verbs (2)

1 **Choose the correct meaning (A, B or C) for each sentence.**

1 Paul may be at football practice.
   A I'm sure that Paul is at football practice.
   B It's possible that Paul is at football practice.
   C It's impossible that Paul is at football practice.
2 It can't be Sam's coat.
   A It's possible that it's Sam's coat.
   B I'm sure it's Sam's coat.
   C It's impossible that it's Sam's coat.
3 It should be fun!
   A I expect it will be fun.
   B I expect it was fun.
   C I don't think it will be fun.
4 We might not get tickets for the concert.
   A I'm sure we won't get tickets.
   B We'll probably get tickets.
   C It's possible that we won't get tickets.
5 She must be very nervous.
   A She definitely isn't very nervous.
   B I'm sure she's very nervous.
   C It's possible that she's very nervous.
6 They could win the competition.
   A It's possible that they will win.
   B They were able to win.
   C It's impossible for them to win.

2 **Choose the correct answers.**

1 I *may*/must go to the party, but I'm not sure yet.
2 No, that *can't*/mustn't be Jed's bike – it's too old!
3 I'd love to go and see that film, but I *might not/couldn't* have time – I've got exams this week.
4 I'm sure she *can/must* feel scared when she has to give a speech.
5 There will be some good speakers, so it *must/should* be interesting.
6 I can't find my purse. *Could/May* it be in your bag?
7 I don't know how much the tickets cost, but they *may not/mustn't* be too expensive.
8 I'm not sure whose bag it is. I suppose it *could/can* be Ana's.

3 **Read the conversation and choose the correct answer, A, B or C.**

Max Are you going to join the debating society?
Lucy I'm not sure. I 1) _____ go along. I think it 2) _____ be interesting.
Max Hmm. I find the idea pretty terrifying, though. I mean, 3) _____ you've got the confidence to speak in front of an audience?
Lucy Yes, I think so. I mean, if you've done your preparation properly, you just get up and speak, don't you? It 4) _____ be that scary!
Max Yes, but it 5) _____ be difficult when people disagree with you.
Lucy I think you worry too much. It 6) _____ be as bad as you think. Why don't we both go along and give it a go?
Max Yes, you 7) _____ be right. OK, I'll come with you!

1	A can	B must	**C** might
2	A should	B must	C can
3	A Could	B Do you think	C Can
4	A can't	B mustn't	C couldn't
5	A might not	B couldn't	C must
6	A may not	B mustn't	C couldn't
7	A can	B could	C should

4 **Rewrite the sentences using the word given. Use between two and five words, including the word given.**

1 I'm sure my bus pass is here somewhere!   **MUST**
   My bus pass _____*must be here*_____ somewhere!
2 It's possible that you won't like the film.   **MIGHT**
   You _____ the film.
3 Is it possible that Jem is ill?   **COULD**
   _____ ill?
4 I'm sure the tickets don't cost that much!   **CAN'T**
   The _____ that much!
5 I expect you will have a wonderful time.   **SHOULD**
   You _____ a wonderful time.
6 Is she a good speaker, in your opinion?   **THINK**
   Do _____ a good speaker?

Reply questions and question tags

5 Choose the correct answers.

1 A I'm going to take part in my first debate next week.
 B *Do you?/*Are you?* Good luck!

2 A It wasn't a very interesting talk.
 B *Was it?/Wasn't it?*

3 A I'll be late to football practice tomorrow.
 B *Will you?/Are you?* Why's that?

4 A I haven't spoken in public before.
 B *Didn't you?/Haven't you?*

5 A She won't win the trophy!
 B *Will she?/Won't she?* Why not?

6 A I'm not very good at giving speeches.
 B *Are you?/Aren't you?* That surprises me.

6 Write reply questions.

1 A All the speeches were really boring!
 B *Were they?* What a pity!

2 A She didn't seem very confident.
 B _____ That's a shame.

3 A It won't matter if we're a bit late.
 B _____ Oh, that's good.

4 A The debate could go on for two hours!
 B _____ That seems like a long time!

5 A My parents helped me prepare my speech.
 B _____ You're lucky!

6 A I'm not interested in that issue.
 B _____ Why not?

7 A Most people weren't listening!
 B _____ How rude!

7 Complete the questions with these question tags. There are two question tags which you don't need.

did they   didn't they   do you   don't you
hasn't he   have you   ~~isn't she~~   shall we
wasn't he   will we

1 Anna's a great speaker, *isn't she* ?
2 You enjoy giving speeches, _____ ?
3 They didn't ask many questions, _____ ?
4 Let's discuss this later, _____ ?
5 Dad was working late last night, _____ ?
6 We won't have time to prepare, _____ ?
7 Your brother's got a lot of friends, _____ ?
8 You've never met Paul, _____ ?

8 Complete the conversation with the correct question tags and reply questions.

Mia I think we should start a debating club at school.

John 1) ___*Do you*___ ? Why's that?

Mia Well, most people of our age are interested in serious issues, 2) _____ ? So, a debating club would encourage them to discuss their ideas, 3) _____ ? Most schools have got debating clubs already.

John 4) _____ ? And are they popular?

Mia Yes, very popular.

John I find that surprising. I mean, most people feel quite shy about speaking in public, 5) _____ ?

Mia That's true. But public speaking can help you to overcome your shyness. Mr Evans talked to us about it last term.

John 6) _____ ? I don't remember that.

Mia Yes. He's quite keen to start a debating club.

John 7) _____ ? OK. Let's go and talk to him then, 8) _____ ?

Revision Unit 12

1 Complete the crossword.

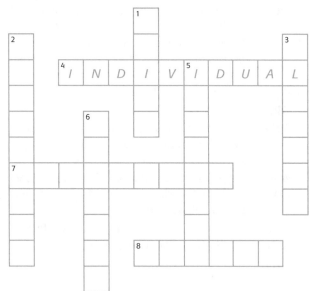

Across row with letters filled: 4 **I N D I V I D U A L**

Across

4 a person

7 writing or words which you can't read

8 a talk that you give in public about a topic

Down

1 the state of being united

2 which you can't see

3 the quality of being clear

5 another word for rude

6 the state of being free

2 Complete the sentences with the correct form of the words in capitals.

1 The secret to exam success is doing enough _preparation_ .   **PREPARE**

2 I thought it was an interesting essay, but I didn't agree with the ....   **CONCLUDE**

3 Jenna and Paula are always having .... about animal rights.   **ARGUE**

4 We had a very interesting .... about climate change.   **DISCUSS**

5 Sometimes Tina behaves in quite a strange, ... way.   **RATIONAL**

6 Cycling without a helmet isn't .... , but it's very foolish!   **LEGAL**

7 Most people would say it's .... to copy homework from other people.   **HONEST**

3 Complete the sentences with these words.

admit   equality   honesty   human rights
respect   responsibility   strength   ~~unity~~

1 Everyone in the club disagrees about this issue – there's no ___unity___ at all!

2 I think it's important to be honest and .... you've made a mistake.

3 It's your .... to feed the cat every day, so don't forget!

4 We encourage our students to have .... for each other and to treat each other fairly.

5 There is a principle of .... before the law, which means that the law treats all citizens in the same way.

6 If you take money that you find to a police station, you may be rewarded for your ....

7 Some governments don't respect the .... of their citizens enough.

4 Complete the text with one word in each space.

Speaker's Corner

Speaker's Corner in London is known as a place where people can speak 1) ___out___ about anything that is on their mind. Londoners take pride 2) .... the fact that many famous people have spoken on this spot, including Karl Marx. Anyone has the right to stand up and talk about anything that they believe 3) .... For example, some people might feel it is important to 4) .... the truth about a political scandal. Others might want to focus 5) .... an environmental issue such as global warming. Whatever your beliefs, Speaker's Corner gives everyone the opportunity to stand 6) .... for their values and feel that they are 7) .... a difference. All you need is to 8) .... plenty of confidence in yourself – and a good loud voice!

5 Choose the correct answer, A, B or C.

1 I'm not sure where Jess is right now. She _____ playing tennis.
   A can be   **B** may be   C must be

2 I'm worried that my team _____ their game.
   A mustn't win   B couldn't win   C may not win

3 I don't know whose bike that is. _____ Tim's?
   A Could it be   B Can it be   C Must it be

4 I'm not sure who the celebrity guest is going to be. It _____ a famous singer.
   A can be   B mustn't   C might be

5 Liam _____ very confident about the exam if he's decided not to do any revision!
   A can be   B must be   C couldn't be

6 That building _____ a school, surely? It's much too small!
   A can't be   B mustn't be   C might not be

7 Why don't you come ice skating with us? It _____ fun!
   A must be   B can be   C should be

8 _____ it's difficult to speak in public?
   A Can you think
   B Do you think
   C Must you think

6 Rewrite the sentences using the word given. Use between two and five words, including the word given.

1 It's possible that I'll be late this evening.   **COULD**
   I _____could be late_____ this evening.

2 I'm sure it's very scary standing up in front of so many people.   **MUST**
   It _____ standing up in front of so many people.

3 It's possible I won't come to the party on Saturday.   **MIGHT**
   _____ to the party on Saturday.

4 It's possible that Stella has a bike that you can borrow.   **MAY**
   Stella _____ that you can borrow.

5 It isn't possible that it's Maria's phone!   **BE**
   It _____ Maria's phone!

6 If we leave at nine, I expect we'll get there by eleven.   **SHOULD**
   If we leave at nine, _____ by eleven.

7 Write reply questions.

1 'I haven't finished yet.'
   '_____*Haven't you?*_____'

2 'The film starts at seven thirty.'
   '_____'

3 'I'll make some pizzas for everyone.'
   '_____ How kind!'

4 'John wasn't very enthusiastic about the idea.'
   '_____'

5 'I can lend you my phone.'
   '_____ That would be great!'

6 'Cara and Jo didn't win their game last night.'
   '_____ That's a shame.'

8 Complete the sentences with the correct question tags.

1 *Mission Impossible* is an American film, _____*isn't it*_____ ?

2 Some governments don't respect human rights, _____ ?

3 Your brother has decided to become a politician, _____ ?

4 Her speech won't be too long, _____ ?

5 You gave your speech yesterday, _____ ?

6 Let's meet at six thirty, _____ ?

9 Complete the conversation with the correct question tags and reply questions.

Leah I'm really nervous about giving my speech.

Josh 1) _____*Are you*_____ ? I don't think you should worry. You've given speeches before, 2) _____ ?

Leah Well, only to my class. I've never given one to the whole school before.

Josh You're going to talk about money and sport, 3) _____ ?

Leah Yes. And I haven't practised it yet!

Josh 4) _____ ? Well, if you want to practise it now, I'll listen to it.

Leah 5) _____ ? That would be great!

Josh No problem. You'll feel much more confident once you've practised, 6) _____ ?

Exam information

The *Cambridge English: First for Schools* is made up of four papers, each testing a different area of ability in English. The Reading and Use of English Paper is worth 40 percent of the marks (80 marks), and each of the other papers is worth 20 percent (40 marks each). There are five grades. A, B and C are pass grades; D and E are fail grades.

Reading and Use of English (1 hour 15 minutes)

Part 1 Multiple-choice cloze	*Focus*	Vocabulary/Lexico grammatical
	Task	You read a text with eight gaps. You choose the best word or phrase to fit in each gap from a set of four options (A, B, C or D).
Part 2 Open cloze	*Focus*	Grammar/Lexico grammatical
	Task	You read a text with eight gaps. You have to think of the best word to fill each gap. No options are provided.
Part 3 Word formation	*Focus*	Vocabulary/Lexico grammatical
	Task	You read a text with eight gaps. You are given the stems of the missing words. You have to change each word to fit the context.
Part 4 Key word transformations	*Focus*	Grammar and vocabulary
	Task	There are six items. You are given a sentence and a 'key word'. You have to complete a second, gapped sentence using the key word. The second sentence has a different grammatical structure but must have a similar meaning to the original.
Part 5 Multiple-choice questions	*Focus*	Detail, opinion, attitude, text organisation features, tone, purpose, main idea, implication, meaning from context.
	Task	There are six four-option multiple-choice questions. You have to choose the correct option (A, B, C or D) based on the information in the text.
Part 6 Gapped text	*Focus*	Understanding text structure, cohesion, coherence
	Task	You read a text from which six sentences have been removed and placed in jumbled order after the text. There is one extra sentence that you do not need to use. You must decide from where in the text the sentences have been removed.
Part 7 Multiple matching	*Focus*	Specific information, detail, opinion and attitude
	Task	You read ten questions or statements and a text which has been divided into sections, or several short texts. You have to decide which section or text contains the information relating to each question or statement.

Writing (1 hour 20 minutes)

The Writing paper has two parts, and you have to complete one task from each part.		
Part 1	*Focus*	Outlining and discussing issues and opinions on a particular topic
	Task	Part 1 is compulsory, and there is no choice of questions. You have to write an essay based on a title and notes. You have to write 140–190 words.
Part 2	*Focus*	Writing a task for a particular purpose based on a specific topic, context and target reader.
	Task	Part 2 has four tasks to choose from which may include: • a letter or email • an article • a report • a review • an essay • a story. The fourth option is based on a set text. You have to write 140–190 words for Part 2.

Listening (approximately 40 minutes)

Part 1 **Extracts with multiple-choice questions**	*Focus*	Each extract will have a different focus, which could be: main point, detail, purpose or location of speech, relationship between the speakers, attitude or opinion of the speakers.
	Task	You hear eight short, unrelated extracts of about thirty seconds each. They may be monologues or conversations. You have to answer one three-option multiple-choice question (A, B or C) for each extract.
Part 2 **Sentence completion**	*Focus*	Specific information, detail, stated opinion
	Task	You hear a monologue or conversation lasting about three minutes. You complete ten sentences with words from the text.
Part 3 **Multiple matching**	*Focus*	Gist, detail, function, attitude, purpose, opinion
	Task	You hear a series of five monologues or exchanges, lasting about thirty seconds each. The speakers in each extract are different, but the situations or topics are all related to each other. You have to match each speaker to one of six statements or questions (A–F). There is one extra option that you do not need to use.
Part 4 **Multiple-choice questions**	*Focus*	Specific information, opinion, attitude, gist, main idea
	Task	You hear an interview or conversation which lasts about three minutes. There are seven questions. You have to choose the correct option (A, B or C).

Speaking (approximately 14 minutes)

You take the Speaking test with a partner. There are two examiners. One is the 'interlocutor', who speaks to you, and the other is the 'assessor', who just listens.

Part 1 **Interview** (3 minutes)	*Focus*	General interactional and social language
	Task	The interlocutor asks each of you questions about yourself, such as where you come from, what you do in your free time.
Part 2 **Individual long turn** (4 minutes)	*Focus*	Organising your ideas, comparing, describing, expressing opinions
	Task	The interlocutor gives you two photographs to compare, and to give a personal reaction to. You speak by yourself for about a minute while your partner listens. Then the interlocutor asks your partner a question related to the topic. Only a short answer is expected. You then change roles.
Part 3 **Collaborative task** (3 minutes)	*Focus*	Interacting with your partner, exchanging ideas, expressing and justifying opinions, agreeing and/or disagreeing, suggesting, speculating, evaluating, reaching a decision through negotiation
	Task	You are given a task to discuss together, based on a set of pictures. You should try to reach a conclusion together, but there is no right or wrong answer to the task, and you don't have to agree with each other. It is the interaction between you that is important.
Part 4 **Discussion** (4 minutes)	*Focus*	Expressing and justifying opinions, agreeing and disagreeing
	Task	The interlocutor asks you both general questions related to the topic of Part 3, and gives you the chance to give your opinions on other aspects of the same topic.

NOTES

Pearson Education Limited
Edinburgh Gate
Harlow
Essex CM20 2JE
England
and Associated Companies throughout the world.

www.pearsonelt.com

© Pearson Education Limited 2015

The right of Sheila Dignen to be identified as authors of this Work has been
asserted by her in accordance with the Copyright, Designs and Patents Act
1988.

First published 2015
Fourth impression 2017

ISBN: 978-1-4479-1391-7

Set in ITC Mixage
Printed in Malaysia, CTP-PJB

Acknowledgements
*The publishers and author would like to thank the following people for their
feedback and comments during the development of the material:*

Elif Berk, Turkey; Alan Del Castillo Castellanos, Mexico; Dilek Kokler,
Turkey; Trevor Lewis, The Netherlands; Nancy Ramirez, Mexico;
Jacqueline Van Mil-Walker, The Netherlands

The publisher would like to thank the following for their kind permission to
reproduce their photographs:

(Key: b-bottom; c-centre; l-left; r-right; t-top)

Alamy Images: blickwinkel 4br, Colin Underhill 17br, Cultura Creative 19cr,
David Grossman 65r, Eddie Gerald 53r, Ersoy Emin 74r, face to face Agentur
GmbH 71r, H. Mark Weidman Photography 68r, Ingram Publishing 73br,
Kumar Sriskandan 42b, Kuttig - Travel 60r, Photofusion Picture Library 70b,
Picture Partners 72r, Relaximages 41 br, Ulrich Doering 43r; **FLPA Images
of Nature:** David Tipling 59r; **Fotolia.com:** Amy Nichole Harris 35r, Enrico
Della Pietra 37r, Ermolaev Alexandr 23r, Mike Lane 62r, Monkey Business
18br, Pink Badger 48r, Ronstik 47r, Tomispin 13br; **Getty Images:** Blend
Images 16l, Carmen MartA-nez BanAs 69r, David Paul Morris 12r, gbh007
44r, Kisgorcs 5br, Phil Boorman 33l; **Glow Images:** Robert Harding 40r;
Pearson Education Ltd: Jon Barlow 9br, Chris Parker 54b, Gareth Boden
29r, 30r, Jules Selmes 25r; **Rex Features:** Adrian Sherratt 31r, Blend Images
66r, Blend Images 66r, John Powell 7cr, Simon Tang 15br; **Shutterstock.
com:** Daniel Prudek 58r, DM7 38b, Dudarev Mikhail 21r, kingfisher 63l,
Lasse Kristensen 51br, Mike Flippo 11br, Noam Armonn 6br; **The Kobal
Collection:** Aardman Animations 64r, Silver Pictures 49br

Cover images: *Front:* **Alamy Images:** TongRo Images

All other images © Pearson Education

Every effort has been made to trace the copyright holders and we apologise
in advance for any unintentional omissions. We would be pleased to
insert the appropriate acknowledgement in any subsequent edition of this
publication.